Mobbed!

Mobbed!

WHAT TO DO WHEN THEY REALLY ARE OUT TO GET YOU

Janice Harper, Ph.D.

©2013, Revised 2016 by Janice Harper, Ph.D. *All rights reserved*

ISBN: 0692693335
ISBN 13: 9780692693339
Library of Congress Control Number: 2016909367
Backdoor Press, Tacoma, Washington

Table of Contents

Foreword

s someone out to get you? Have they made things so bad for you that now *a lot* of people are out to get you? Have your friends or coworkers been told to avoid you, and one-by-one they've obliged? Are you being accused of everything from moral failings to criminal behavior?

If so, you need some information and you need some help. In this book, I go where a lot of the anti-bully books will not go—into the minds of good people who will *become* bullies when given the opportunity—and into your own confused mind when under attack and making bad decisions.

I will take you through the labyrinth of lies, distortions, and smear campaigns that commence when a bully turns into a mob—and you find yourself the subject of gossip, lies, inquisitions and accusations from the very people you once trusted as friends, coworkers, and colleagues. I'll tell you how to cope, with a few dirty tricks and a few uncomfortable truths. And I'll tell you how to start to heal once the attacks have stopped, but the wounds still bleed.

Why The Bully Label Isn't Going to Help You

When I found myself under attack at work—falsely accused of one bad thing after another, my reputation and achievements smeared or credited to others, shunned by my closest friends and colleagues and eventually run out of my job as a professor and my twenty-year profession in anthropology when I was ultimately accused of acts of nuclear terrorism—hey, why not, it didn't matter if there was a shred of truth to it, the scandal was all that it took—I turned to the books on bullies. And a lot of what I read made sense. But a lot of it made me tremble.

I trembled a lot back then. I was an emotional wreck from the gossip, the shunning, the accusations and the constant investigations—some open and transparent, for all the world to scrutinize, others so secret I didn't know about them until they were over and the lawyers got involved. I was living proof that cruel people could reduce a strong and healthy person to a puddle of fear and emotion, and could and would destroy families and lives. But when I read what some of these books were recommending, I knew it was only a matter of time before more lives and careers were destroyed in the name of ridding the workplace of "bullies."

Why? Why did the anti-bully books that had helped me also bother me? Because so much of what was recommended was either precisely what I had done—report it, talk to others about it, file a lawsuit—all of which only made the situation far worse and far more damaging. Or what was recommended was exactly what was happening *to* me—tell people that the person you want out is a problem, get others to share their experiences, keep a record of everything they do to annoy you, avoid them, do not cooperate with them at work, refuse to work with them, ensure they never work again. That wasn't just bullying—that was mobbing—collective bullying done with the approval of management. And that was wrong—no matter who was the target. If the answer to bullying was to start mobbing, I wanted no part of it.

I'd first heard about mobbing when a colleague from grad school blew the whistle on a disturbing report on water quality that his employer—a county public health agency—had suppressed. The next thing he knew, my friend was being called crazy and dangerous and he was forced out of his job. He called his experience "mobbing" and explained that it was a phenomenon that has long been recognized in Europe, and involves an entire group of people ganging up on someone. I'd heard how quickly it had intensified at his job, and seen what it had done to him, and filed the term "mobbing" in the back of my head as "useful information," something to keep an eye out for in case it ever happened to me.

But I didn't recognize it happening to me until it was too late. That was because I thought my friends and coworkers were different. I thought they were good people (and many of them are, although we are no longer friends or colleagues); I thought that they would fight for the principles they displayed on their bumper stickers (none did, though I have no doubt they have convinced themselves they did by having collectively demonized me), and I thought for the longest time that my problem was "bullies"— the bad people.

What I did not see clearly was that focusing on the "bullies" made it impossible for me to see what was going on with those around me who were not "bullies." What I did not see or understand was that group psychology operates very differently from individual psychology—and that I hadn't stood a chance when I opened my big mouth and fought for "principles."

I also realized as I read those books on bullies that it was only a matter of time before my employer said that I was a bully. Not because of anything I did or said; indeed, my record prior to my mobbing was fine, and I was described as "well respected" by my students, "warm and welcoming" to my peers, and just two months before my mobbing, "indispensible" to my department. But because the social tides had turned against bullies, I knew that if my employers wanted to undermine my support outside the workplace, all they had to do was say I was a bully. If they started calling me a bully, no one would care about me anymore, and they would be the victims, not me. And I knew that if my employers started calling me a bully, the call for me to be eradicated from the workplace would be complete and done in the name of social progress—because there is zero tolerance for "bullies."

It was years before they slapped the bully label on me, however, and long after I had sued them and they had paid me a substantial six figure settlement to drop my lawsuit. In the meantime, I had begun to make a name for myself in the anti-bully field for sharing my concerns and writing about mobbing. I am a cultural anthropologist and before my career was so cruelly cut down among my specializations were organizational cultures, and warfare and structural violence.

It was when I was teaching a course on genocide as I battled my employers that I began to discern that many of the same psychological processes that enable autocratic leaders to persuade entire populations to turn on their neighbors and mutilate and kill them, are the same psychological processes that happen in the workplace when autocratic managers persuade their workforce to turn against a coworker. Clearly the consequences of the two processes are profoundly different—in genocide people are physically tortured and killed and forced to endure unspeakable atrocities, whereas in the group aggression of "mobbing" the wounding is quite different. Mobbing is still a form of psychological torture and it still kills, but on a far different end of the spectrum of violence.

But the group psychology that makes each act of collective aggression possible is nearly identical—a person (or in the case of genocide, group of people) is viewed as fundamentally different from the rest of the group; their "difference" is communicated to others and in time, meaning is conferred on that difference to suggest they are inferior to the rest of the group; they are targeted for elimination from the group by someone in a position of power; they are increasingly excluded from the social sphere and strategic resources; they are isolated and called names to dehumanize them (making it easier to harm them); they are increasingly described as a threat to the group; and the rest of the group learns that they could become targets themselves if they align with the target, but that they could benefit if they help leadership get rid of them. Soon, virtually everyone shares the view that the targeted person or "sub-group" is deserving of the bad treatment, and should be eliminated—no matter what it takes.

Shortly after identifying these similar processes between genocide and mobbing, I wrote a piece called, *Just Us Justice: The Gentle Genocide of Workplace Mobbing* which was published in an ebook by Anton Hout, *What Every Target of Workplace Bullying Needs to Know*. Soon after it was published I began hearing from mobbing targets regularly, who shared their experiences and asked for help. I began writing on the topic for *The Huffington Post* and *Psychology Today*, and received even more pleas for help—along with some surprising attacks.

One of the leading anti-bully writers wrote a forceful blog post attacking me, calling me a naïve young Pollyanna and urging people not to pay any attention to me. When he finally met me at a public talk, he began screaming at me, jabbing his finger in the air at me while turning beat red in rage. Finally, he turned around and bent over and lifted his suit coat in a gesture to kiss his ass—all for having asked if the term "bully" was a form of name calling itself.

Another leading anti-bully figure wrote that after reading what I wrote, he understood why my coworkers had mobbed me. Vicious comments were left on my published essays, and soon I began receiving emails threatening to harm me, including posting my home address and suggesting people go to my home and beat me up, while some even said I should be raped. The attacks from some of these "anti-bully" writers were every bit if not more aggressive than much of the bullying I'd endured in the workplace. And like the mobbing I had endured, they were done by people who believed they were not "bullying" because I "deserved it." They believed they were not bullying me because they were not "bullies." And they believed that they were not being aggressive because they viewed me as the aggressor—for having disagreed in print and expressed a different view I was "fighting" them.

It wasn't long after that, just as I expected, my former employers finally got around to slapping the bully label on me—over two years after settling my lawsuit. I'd been contacted by a reporter who wanted to interview me for the local paper in the town where I'd worked as a university professor.

She said she wanted to interview me as a target and as an expert. But it was clear that she had a poor grasp of the concept. She kept speaking about "bullies," while I tried to explain that I don't write about "bullies," because that's name-calling and labeling a person. When we label a person, we stop seeing them. It's sort of like that optical illusion—one moment you see a beautiful woman, but when someone points out that she's really a witch, that's all we ever see in the picture again. Every time we catch a glimpse of the beautiful woman, our minds instantly shift back to the wicked witch.

Well the bully label is a lot like that. It stops us from seeing the person before us. It also stops us from seeing the behavior—we see instead the expected behavior, what we have been taught "bullies" do. But in reality, human behavior is far more nuanced, and humans are complex. Yes, some are the stereotypical bullies—I would certainly lump that anti-bully expert in with that group. But others are people trying to cope when under a lot of stress. And some don't realize how their behavior is perceived by others, but if made aware, are open to changing.

In other words, when people are out to get us, it doesn't help to think of them as "bullies." By focusing on "bullies" we find ourselves sorting people into the good and bad piles of our minds. We focus on the psychology of how individual people behave, which means we aren't paying any attention at all to group psychology. We end up blindsided by the aggression of all those "good" people. And a focus on "bullies" lets all the others off the hook—the good, decent people who behave brutally when told by leadership to do so.

When that reporter was asking me why I didn't like to call people bullies, I told her that one of my concerns with the label is that it is the perfect weapon for an abusive employer to use against an employee they want out—by calling them a bully, people will stop caring. Anything goes. There's zero tolerance for bullies, so all that an employer who wants to be rid of a good employee has to do to defend their abusive actions and mobbing behavior is to say they were protecting the workplace from bullies.

But she didn't believe me. She said she found it hard to believe that would ever happen, but she was looking forward to interviewing me. And then I didn't hear back from her.

A few weeks later, I sent her an email asking what was up and she replied that she wouldn't be using me as a source after having spoken to my former employer. Curious, I asked why.

Because they said I was a bully.

I knew it was pointless to counter that not only was I not a bully, I had never, not even in the heat of the mobbing, been accused of being one. Nonetheless, she would still not include my story; what had happened to me no longer mattered.

Well, then, I said, how about using me as an expert, as you'd planned?

No thank you.

That's how it goes. That was the very first time I'd ever had the bully label slapped on me, and I later learned that when the reporter contacted my attorney, my attorney assured her that "bully" was the last thing I could be honestly called (and believe me, my attorney had seen the very worst of me), but it didn't matter. Once the label had been slapped on me, my story no longer mattered.

I had tried to tell my story in the past, and I found that people didn't believe it. It was too outlandish, too bizarre. Somehow the worse my employer and coworkers behaved toward me, the more the perception shifted from what they were doing to me, to what I had done to deserve it.

After awhile, I stopped telling my story, because it no longer mattered. I'd heard hundreds of stories, and while few went as far as mine—investigated and exonerated by four levels of law enforcement, including Homeland Security—and few lost as much as I had—the pattern was always the same with almost everyone I spoke with. They'd been liked and respected at work (or church or school or in the military or wherever), when something happened and it all suddenly changed. Their roles had been significantly diminished. They were accused of something, often many things, and forced to endure endless and exhausting investigations and reviews.

Hurtful rumors were circulating and people they cared about were shunning them. They were facing the loss of their job, and most were over forty-five and unlikely to find comparable work. In many cases, losing a job meant moving—and losing a home. Almost all had had to see attorneys, and many were involved in lawsuits or contemplating one. Marriages were ending, children were traumatized, and the money was running out.

My own story didn't matter all that much, once I realized that so many people had lived through their own version of it. What I saw happening was a patterned process as predictable as physics. And the wounds we suffered were the same—profound grief, rage, confusion, sadness, depression, fear, suicidal thoughts. Friends and family were doing their best to understand, but even they didn't really understand. They didn't understand the obsessive thinking about what had happened, how it happened, and what could or was going to happen. They didn't understand how it could happen if there wasn't something the person had done to bring it on. They just saw someone they cared about falling apart, and not getting any better.

People who have been the target of group aggression want help and they want it fast. They're scared. They're frantic. And they're increasingly alone as they battle the rumors and lies and accusations that seem to come from everywhere as their lives and careers unravel in a sudden and seemingly inexplicable onslaught. They aren't being bullied. They're being mobbed.

What This Book is All About

The book that follows is a straight-shot at the problem, as I do my best to explain mobbing in a nutshell. Although I refer primarily to the workplace, almost all of what I discuss can be applied to any group setting where someone is the target of collective aggression.

I don't pull any punches and I don't spare the target—all of us have a lot to learn about changing our own behaviors. All of us. And there's no more critical time to do that than when you're being mobbed. If people are out to get you, it doesn't mean that you deserve it. But what it does mean is you have to look at yourself—with tenderness, with compassion, and with love, but you have to look at yourself as clearly, as honestly, and as tenderly brutally as possible—if you're going to survive the mob. Because the mob won't ever look at itself. The mob won't change its behaviors. The mob won't apologize. But the mob can, however cruelly, teach you lessons about yourself and how you relate to people, lessons that you need to know. And the mob can destroy you, if you don't understand yourself—or understand how the mob itself operates and grows.

I don't have all the answers, but I do have *some* answers. As with any social problem, there are a number of different approaches that can be taken, and this one is mine, based on my expertise as an anthropologist specializing in organizational cultures and in warfare. It is based on years of research on the topics of bullying and mobbing, on individual and group psychology, on group aggression, on management practices, and on how workers are taught to get ahead at work. It is based on interviews, conversations, and emails with over a three hundred mobbing and bullying targets, shunned workers, and experts in the field of bullying and mobbing. And it is based on my own experiences of having been viciously mobbed, including by people I cared deeply about and had gone to great lengths to help in their own careers.

As I was preparing this book for publication and read over some of the passages I wrote in the pages that follow, I laughed at how obvious it is that some sections reflect my own frustrations and rage at the ordeal I endured when I was mobbed. But I left many of those passages in because they are consistent with what others have described to me of their own experiences, and because I want the human side of mobbing to live in the pages that follow. Mobbing is enraging. It is devastating. And it is incredibly surreal and Kafkaesque. I want the reader to feel that madness, to know that mobbing isn't just a matter of people being rude. Mobbing is far more than that.

Mobbing is bullying run amuck and it is cruel and inhumane. But as I show in these pages, it is also human. And because it is human, it cannot be stopped. But it can be better understood, and if it is better understood, it is my hope that fewer people will get caught up in it when one of their co-workers or a member of their group is targeted. It is my hope that everyone who reads this book will think twice before gossiping about someone who is under attack, will think twice about shunning them, and will think twice about attacking them even further.

Mobbing targets don't need any more attacks; they need help. And if there is any way that I can help someone who is being put through the social gauntlet of mobbing, then I want to do so. This little book is a start, and while it doesn't have any magic answers or solutions, it does have many tools for minimizing the aggression, safeguarding against further attacks, and protecting yourself and your career.

Because ultimately, if you are being mobbed, that is what you need to do. It doesn't matter how wrong, unjust or even illegal the actions of your employer and coworkers may be. What matters is that you survive—and eventually, flourish.

So with those thoughts in mind, pour yourself a warm or cool drink, find a comfortable spot and read on. If you are being bullied or mobbed, remember, you're safe, right now, this moment. Embrace this moment, and give my words some thought. I promise you, you'll find some tips or insights well worth knowing. I learned them the hard way; I want you to learn them the easy way. All you need to do is listen.

Introduction

I t seems you can't turn on the TV or go to a website these days without hearing about bullies. Cartoonish images of screaming tyrants with smoke shooting out of their ears, fire flying off serpentine tongues or monstrous children stealing some little kid's lunch money illustrate the brutish aggression of bullying in most of what we read about bullying. And in telling us how to cope with bullies, the message to the "victim" is clear: if you're being bullied it's because you're *too* good, they're jealous of you, and because of them you'll suffer such profound PTSD that you'll need psychiatric care for the rest of your life.

The remedy all too often recommended: bullies should be branded, exiled, sued and publicly shamed. But is that so bad? Let's face it, if you are the target of someone's irrational aggression, whether at work, school or in your community, that sentiment is exactly what you want to hear. Because to have someone come after you can be a devastating experience. It can and does demoralize people, reduce them to tears, make them feel like crap, destroy their reputation, and even drive some to suicide, if not homicide.

Given all that, what's wrong with going after bullies? What's wrong is this: trite as it sounds, you can't change anyone else's behavior; you can only change your own. And there's another reason, maybe even more important: bullying snowballs into mobbing very quickly. Once it does, the people who will do you the most harm won't be "the bullies." They will be your friends and coworkers. And how is it going to sound if you alone point to half the workforce and say they're *all* bullies? You'll sound crazy.

What's happening when a whole bunch of people turn on you is called mobbing. Mobbing is group bullying run amuck where you are shunned, sabotaged, and put through the system with a series of bad reviews, passed opportunities, warnings, gossip and accusations that often lead to investigations and inquisitions that can ultimately destroy your career.

Mobbing is *group* aggression, and it is distinct from bullying because the people who engage in it include not only "bullies," but once supportive, friendly, non-aggressive people who have suddenly been encouraged to see you as a threat.

When that happens, the person who is ultimately driven out will not necessarily be the most aggressive or abusive. **The person who will be branded, exiled and publicly shamed as "the problem" and maybe even as "the bully" is always the person who has the least amount of power**. And that person could very well be you, if someone's out to get you.

So I'm going to tell you how someone who doesn't like you can mobilize a group for a united attack against you; how group aggression works; and how you can save yourself if a group is out to get you.

As I do so, I'm going to challenge some common views about "bullies" and their "victims." But I'm not going to challenge these views because I support bullies or because I think they're no big deal. Bullying is indeed a big deal and the consequences are profound. I'm going to challenge these views because I think they fuel aggression, provide new tools and techniques for destroying people, and disempower targets by telling them comforting lies.

Just what are some of these lies?

- That bullies are psychopaths;
- That bullies are bad people;

- That destroying and eliminating bullies is a good thing, done by good people;
- That once the bully is gone the problem is resolved;
- That if you *think* you're being bullied, then you *are* being bullied;
- That if you're being bullied at work, you must be an excellent employee;
- That if you're under attack, you did nothing to bring it on;
- And that all you need is a lawsuit, and the bully will pay, while you can get your life back.

These are myths and lies. And if you believe them, you will either remain a victim, too disabled to work again or too unaware of your own flaws and social reactions that you will be unable to grow and change constructively from this horrible experience. You may even become an aggressor yourself, excusing your bad behavior because you've come to believe the target of your wrath deserved it, if you are convinced they are a "bully."

Instead, I'm going to tell you that yes, there are people who are nasty and mean spirited and who will take great delight in tormenting and humiliating people, and that they are very often in positions of leadership and they may totally mess with your life and it's wrong.

But I'm also going to tell you that **as long as they are in a position of leadership, they are in a position of influence over other people**. And that means that it takes very little for them to get these other people to turn against you, no matter what your reputation was before the attacks or how good those people are to you in normal situations.

I am going to tell you that by the time you realize that the "bully" has been cozying up to your friends, coworkers, clients, colleagues and others, it will probably be too late. They will have poisoned your reputation and created a very dark filter through which others view you. I am going to tell you that it doesn't matter what a person says, thinks or even writes about social justice or worker rights or discrimination or morals or religion, **there is no correspondence between people's ideological views and their**

actions when they are behaving in a group. Worse, there may even be an inverse relationship and the more strongly people view themselves as moral, the more likely they will justify their attacks against you as deserved.

I am going to tell you that the closer these people are to you—as a friend, or as a member of a similarly situated class—such as having the same gender, age, politics, sexuality, what have you—*the more likely* they will turn against you—and the more damaging they will become when they do.

I am going to tell you that filing complaints and lawsuits can be a professional death sentence, even if you're right, and even if you win. I am going to tell you that the more outrageous and untrue the things they say about you, the more likely they will be believed. I am going to tell you that until and unless you can control your emotions—at a time when you are emotionally overwhelmed and shattered—that you will be considered crazy and the aggression against you will be considered justified and it will get worse.

And I am going to tell you that there are specific things you can do, or should not to, to control the aggression, manage the mob, and keep an eye on the backstabbers and jackals who are likely to do you in.

I cannot promise you that if you follow my advice that the bullying and mobbing will stop. I cannot even promise you that things will get better. Because they just might get worse. But what I can promise you is if you listen and consider what I have to say in these pages, you will have another way of seeing the problem that just might help you out in ways that other strategies have not. I can promise you that the more you understand the difference between individual behavior and group behavior, the better your chances of limiting the aggression—and recognizing when it's brewing. And I can promise you that you will have far fewer surprises and shocks along the way.

Now you are probably skeptical, and may even be screaming at me this very moment, howling that I just don't understand what it's like to be bullied. But rest assured I do. I know just how bad it feels to have a bully lead a mob, to be put down, humiliated, falsely accused, shunned and driven into such despair and anguish that you'd rather they just tie you to a post and peel off your skin than continue to destroy you with their acts and words.

I know what it feels like to desperately try to save your job, only to lose not only the job, but your reputation, your privacy, your dignity, your friends, your career, your home, your pension, your assets and your sanity. And then to file a lawsuit. And settle that lawsuit for a hefty settlement that does nothing to make you whole, leaves you virtually unemployable late in life with a child to support and no living family to help you out, and watch as that settlement goes to the lawyers, the IRS, the debts from long-term unemployment, and then eventually it's gone and not a soul will hire you.

Because that's what bullying did to me—despite having a stellar reputation and work record beforehand. *So I get it.* But I also think that some of the anti-bullying experts are giving some very bad advice, and doing more to promote workplace aggression, than to promote workplace compassion.

Another thing I know is that for all that I have suffered as a result of bullying, I am healthier mentally, spiritually and physically (give or take an ossifying bone or shedding brain cell) than I was before I endured a mobbing. And I am far wiser, more compassionate, and more at peace than I ever was, because I have learned as much about myself as I have about others. That doesn't mean the mobbing I endured was okay by any means, nor that it was justified. It was neither. But it means that I have not been destroyed because of it, and have instead grown from it.

I have written this book as a step toward promoting greater compassion and civility in the workplace and in any community in which humans come together as a group. It is one small step toward trying to help targets of group aggression find a safer and saner way to cope and overcome the brutality of bullying, mobbing and shunning.

Who This Book Is For

This book is for anyone who has found themselves mistreated, abused, put down, sabotaged, or humiliated by someone *in a group setting of adults*, whether by a boss, coworker, teacher, or anyone else who is making your life hell. Although I focus primarily on the workplace, you may find yourself mobbed not just at work, but at college, at church, in your family, in your neighborhood, or even at your country club.

It is written for anyone who is being mobbed or bullied by a group, gossiped about, or shunned. It is for anyone who has been excluded from a group they once belonged to, and this exclusion is having a significant impact on their lives or livelihoods.

It is written for anyone who has been unjustly accused of misconduct, sexual harassment, breaking the law, violating ethics, or even accused of bullying, and as a result has been put through a series of investigations, tribunals and smear campaigns.

And it is written for the bystander, whose own life is being turned to hell by someone else's problem. Who wants to help but doesn't know how. Who has been told that someone they live or work with has done something really wrong and as crazy as it sounds, so many people are saying it that they don't know what to think.

It is *not* written for the person who believes they are being followed from city to city unless they happen to be a scandal-ridden superstar or a whistleblower of super-secrets and worked for the CIA. If you have left your job and are not involved with a lawsuit, the shunning and professional smears may persist, but if you think they're still following you in the streets, sneaking into your home while you're gone to rearrange your furniture, or harassing you through the light sockets, get help.

It is *not* written for the person who doesn't have many friends and finds themselves shut out of things, but their career is fine, no one is trying to have them fired, no one is sabotaging their work and they are invited to all formal work-related social events. If this is your situation, you are just unpopular. But do take a good hard look within because if it persists you just may end being mobbed. Until then, if you find people avoiding you but there is no interest from your organizational leadership in trying to get rid of you, change your own behaviors. Be friendlier, cooperate with your coworkers, don't complain, and show some compassion and empathy toward others and less concern about yourself. Listen more, bitch less. Then things should get better. If they don't, maybe it's just not a friendly place to work. Move on or accept it, but don't confuse an unfriendly workplace with being mobbed. Once you've been mobbed, "unfriendly" were the good ol' days.

It is *not* written for the person who is being shunned because he or she has knowingly violated the trust of their community or other people. If you are a sexual predator, well, own up to it. If you really did embezzle the money, get a lawyer. People are avoiding you not because of what they think you did, but because of what you actually did. There's a difference.

But what if you did stretch the boundaries with an inappropriate comment or momentary temper tantrum, but now the reaction to your bad behavior is going way, way overboard and you are being treated like a pariah for something that could just as easily have been resolved with a closed door conversation? Then this handbook will be helpful, but as you'll read, you still need to take a good long look in the mirror and accept the penalty for your conduct. But that doesn't mean that anyone has any right to destroy you.

What if you really did bully someone? Same thing. Own up to it. And stop it. But that doesn't mean you deserve to be dehumanized and accused of ever-escalating atrocities you never did commit. And it doesn't mean you deserve to be so subjected to inquisition that you can't get any work done or can't get another job once they fire you. And it doesn't mean that you are only what they say you are. But it does mean you've got issues.

We all do. And sometimes the line between acceptable and unacceptable behavior is a fine one. Other times it's as clear as a barbed-wire fence. If you fire an employee for not sleeping with you, you have violated someone else and you have been cruel for the sake of your own ego. On the other hand, if you made inappropriate comments, should you be treated like a rapist? No. But you very well might be.

If I sound a bit confusing about who this book is or is not for, that's because human behavior is not black and white; it's ambiguous. It's even more confusing when humans act together in a group. Group behavior revises people's social identities and rewrites their histories, creating ever-more-spectacular accusations as it gains momentum. Group behavior just gets weirder and weirder until no one involved has any idea what really happened, but they just want the problem gone.

Unfortunately, "the problem" is all too often a person. And that person is not necessarily the one who instigated or enflamed the conflict, and may well not even be the one who did anything wrong at all. The person to go will be the one the mob decides must go—the one with the least amount of power, the one accused by the person with the most power, the one in the wrong place, at the wrong time, the one who fights the hardest when the wheels of injustice start to churn.

In other words, it doesn't matter whether you did anything wrong, or did everything right. It doesn't matter if the person coming after you is a bully or an obedient cog just doing their job. It doesn't matter if you have a pristine work record or you've made mistakes. We all make mistakes. What matters is they're out to get you, unjustly. And once that happens, you need to be prepared. So I'm here to prepare you with the cold, hard reality of what happens once a bully turns into a mob, and to share some ideas on how you can protect yourself once that happens.

Organization of the Book

The book is divided into two parts. The first part is an overview of what mobbing is and how it unfolds. The second part focuses on what you can do to manage it. If you're being mobbed, you want help fast. But as eager as you may be to learn what you can do to manage it, I encourage you to read the first part first. The more you understand the process, the better prepared you will be to manage it.

To get started, I want to get you thinking about how animals treat each other. Because when we're scared we don't think straight. When we're scared we revert to our Homo sapiens nature which is to say, we act like animals. That goes not just for you, but for all the people around you and who might be after you. Everyone is acting like an animal because that's what humans are. So understanding something about our animal nature may help us to understand how the group will respond when one animal—one that is bigger and meaner and has some clout—sets its sights on another animal—you.

Every species has its bullies, that aggressive individual who will hiss and bite and chase another of its own kind far away. But humans are one of the few species that will *organize* its members into a group to attack another of its members. To paraphrase the Cole Porter song, birds do it, ants do it, even chimpanzees in the zoo do it. But this is no love song; I'm talking here about intra-species warfare—going to war with your own kind.

So we'll start by giving some thought to our animal nature, which I think is much more revealing than sorting people into good guys and bad guys, or bullies and victims. By understanding our animal nature, we are less prone to misjudging people. We misjudge people when we expect them to behave a certain way because we know they are otherwise good or otherwise bad or because they have principles that we think will lead them to do the right thing or that we fear will lead them to the wrong thing. **When people behave in groups, their animal nature will almost always prevail over their personal nature**. Those who defy the group to defend another under attack are rare, and they are usually not the people we expect they will be.

So we start by looking at animals because when mobbing gets underway, the people involved will not respond from a rational standpoint. Logic won't work in responding to them because their animal natures will prevail, which doesn't make them any less responsible for their actions. It just makes it easier to survive them.

You can skip the chapter on animal behavior if you want, but I really urge you to read it. Read it with these questions in mind—What does it tell me about how people will behave if they get scared? What can I learn from it the next time I find myself in a group of people? And what does it tell me about myself—as an aggressor (for we all exhibit aggression at one time or another) and as a target of group aggression? What can learning about the nature of animals tell me about human nature? If you keep these thoughts in mind, by the time we get to the other chapters, you'll find yourself looking at conflict in a different way—less judgmentally, perhaps, and more observantly. Because **judging bad behavior does nothing to spare you from it. If you want to survive it, observe it.**

Then I'm going to talk about organizational cultures, and how people position themselves for power, respond to power, or negotiate for power. I'm going to talk about how power is used from the top on down, to how those on the bottom take advantage of conflict to climb to the top. It will sound an awful lot like rhesus monkey behavior, you'll discover.

Once you understand how animals behave and how organizations operate, it's time to get to the way mobbing starts in the early stage. It's something that happens to the organizational culture when someone, for whatever reason, triggers an administrative investigation or, as novelist Philip Roth has described it, "the incident." I'm going to talk about what happens behind the scenes when "an incident" transpires, about who picks up the phone or drops a thought into someone's head and how they do it, about how decisions about the outcome are actually made. Remember those animals? Well, this is the werewolf stage, when perfectly ordinary people suddenly start howling at the moon—right before they sink their fangs into you and tear you limb from limb.

Once the werewolf starts howling, it's only a matter of time before all the other creatures in the woods prick up their ears and start making some decisions. They want to know what is going on, they aren't quite certain what it is, but they know someone is going to shed some blood. First to come out are the jackals. This is where we give some thought to gossip, rumor and eye witness accounts. Why do your friends believe the ugly rumors that get told about you, especially at a time when you are so clearly in need of their support? Often it's because the person telling the rumor believes it even if they're lying. And how they come to believe it has far less to do with what actually happened or even how conceivable it is, *than with how others are behaving and which perception is most useful.*

This is how Joseph Goebbels was able to help Adolf Hitler come to power, why Joseph McCarthy was able to persuade so many people to turn their coworkers, friends, family members and neighbors over to the FBI with claims they were communists, why in the mid 1980's so many daycare workers were accused of impossible feats of sexual perversity and sent to prison with no evidence, and why so many people throughout the globe have been burned and hung as witches. Understanding how rumors, gossip and outright lies turn into social hysteria will help you to understand how the unbelievable can become believable if someone comes after you no matter what the century or who the people. Knowing how that process operates early on can spare you from becoming the subject of irrational gossip or even worse, flat out accused.

Then I'm going to tell you about what really goes on in internal investigations, who gets interviewed and how (and who doesn't), what questions get asked and which ones don't get asked, what findings get found and how evidence gets collected. If what you think is that all you need to do is state the facts, produce some emails, hand over the diary you've been keeping about all the abuse you've suffered, and you'll be vindicated, think again.

If you are being mobbed, you will be sucked into the vortex of institutional investigations, and no matter what the facts are, you will be found either guilty of the claims against you or of having lied about any claims you have against anybody else (very often both). You may have no choice but to participate in what you know is a predetermined inquisition, so you're going to need to understand how they work, and how you can best stay sane and safe when in the midst of one. Internal investigations are to mobbing what condoms are to orgies. They protect the pricks and help everyone to fuck you without any worries of the consequences.

Once you understand how group aggression operates and how a bully can turn into a mob, you will be ready to learn what you can do to protect against it. In Part Two, I'll tell you how to recognize and respond to aggressive behavior at an early stage by diffusing it at best, and avoiding it if you must. I will tell you how and why to put up and shut up even when every fiber of your flesh and every cell of your soul tells you that to ignore it is just wrong. I will explain why and how you can grow emotionally, psychologically and spiritually by letting go of pain and rage early on, even when the other person is behaving like a monster.

And then, when you've ignored me (because you probably will; I know because I never would have listened when I was going through it), I will tell you how to lay low and how to monitor the action behind the scenes—the emails that are circulated, the gossip networks that are formed. I will explain what to make note of in your journal or calendar and what not to put down. I will tell you how to take notes in such a manner that if it ever does come to a lawsuit, you will be prepared. And I will tell you how and why to contact the EEOC and/or an attorney, and why you probably shouldn't.

And then I'm going to tell you how to save your career and save your sanity, because I lost both of mine, and now know what went wrong and why. As pilot Chesley Sullenberger, better known as "Sully," the U.S. Airways pilot who steered his crashing jet to heroic safety has noted, every safety regulation we have, every improvement that has ever been made in industrial, workplace or transportation safety has come about because somebody died. Well let me tell you, as one who was assassinated and left bleeding in my grave, it's no place to be.

Let me help you get through this process more safely and more sanely. Let me help you avoid the landmines I didn't just step on, but the ones I pounced up and down on in all my righteous rage. I had every right to be angry when I was mobbed. But I also had every right to be safe. So do you, and in the pages that follow I show you a way to make that happen.

With those thoughts in mind, I ask of you only this one grace: just because I'll talk about mistakes you may be making to enflame the mob, don't assume I think it is okay that this is happening to you. It is not okay. It's inhumane and cruel and completely unnecessary and stupid. But if it is happening, *none of that matters.* What matters is that inhumanity and cruelty and unnecessary stupidity happen all the time, and sometimes it's incomprehensible how quickly and how viciously it goes down. The more you comprehend this discomforting reality, the more likely you'll master not just the situation, but your soul. And isn't that more important than screaming about what's wrong with bullies? They've got their own souls to save; you take care of yours—so that they can't destroy it.

PART I

Making Sense of it All

CHAPTER 1

How Animals Treat Each Other

For all the talk of bullying, it remains viewed as something bad people do. But when a bully turns into a mob, everyone gets in on the act—even good people. For that reason, it pays to understand what mobbing is, and how it progresses from an individual bullying jerk, to a venomous, vicious mob of good people gone bad.

Konrad Lorenz was a 20th century Austrian zoologist who coined the term "mobbing" to refer to group aggression after watching the behavior of birds. Heinz Leymann, a German-Swedish psychologist, applied Lorenz's findings about bird behavior to human aggression, noting that how humans attack each other at work is very similar to the mobbing behavior that Lorenz had noted among birds.

Lorenz noticed that when a lone and unfamiliar bird or predator strays into the territory of a group of birds, other birds will join in and circle the intruder, swooping and swooning, striking the intruder repeatedly with hard, swift blows. These blows are not lethal at first—their intent is to scare off the intruder. If the intruder remains, the blows will increase until the intruder is slightly injured. The attacking birds will fly off momentarily, but then return, watching, following, and encircling the injured bird. If it still does not leave, the birds will become more aggressive, swooping down again, grazing, drawing blood, retreating, circling, again and again.

But one of the most fascinating behaviors that Lorenz discovered was that the longer an avian attack goes on, the more the onlookers turn into aggressors. When other birds pass by, birds with no interest in the matter whatsoever and under no threat from the prey at all, they will join in the attacks. The birds will continue to escalate their attacks until the bloodied prey crawls off too weakened to ever rise again. Or until it falls down and dies.

Birds do not usually attack other *flocks* of birds, however. Birds will strategically organize as a group to attack, but the group will attack only individuals, not other flocks. What Lorenz found so fascinating about this behavior is that it is precisely the type of behavior we see among humans when they are living or working together as a group. The vulnerable lone intruder will be perceived as a threat, and the flock will gather and swoop and peck away until the intruder is incapacitated, dead or out of site. They'll literally mob the intruder.

No one has captured the mob violence of birds better than Alfred Hitchcock, in his classic film, *The Birds*.

"Seems like a pattern, doesn't it?" Mitch Brenner, the film's leading man observes. "They strike, then disappear, and then start massing again."

Brenner is perplexed by the aggressive behavior of gulls, ravens and crows as the birds gather in swarms, circling the tranquil fishing village of Bodega Bay, California. The birds become increasingly aggressive and destructive as they descend, diving and attacking the innocent villagers until a constant sense of fear and dread permeates the community, a community in fear not just of the birds, but of anyone who does not belong in their solitary, grounded world.

The birds' aggression coincided with the arrival of a beautiful blonde stranger, Miss Melanie Daniels. Miss Daniels is a mink-draped socialite who has come from her home of San Francisco to Bodega Bay on a whim, in pursuit of romance with the handsome attorney, Mitch Brenner. After a particularly brutal attack by the birds, Brenner and Daniels find shelter inside a restaurant where others are huddled, seeking refuge from the birds. But as soon as they enter the local diner thinking they are safe from attack, a furious woman bursts from the group, singling out Miss Daniels, to accuse her of being the cause of the birds' aggression.

"*Why* are they doing this? *Why* are they doing this?" the woman, a young mother, screams, "They said when *you* got here, the whole thing started. *Who* are you? *What* are you? Where did you come from? I think *you're* the cause of all this. I think you're evil! *EVIL!*"

Melanie Daniels is, after all, different from most people in the town, openly displaying her wealth and wiles while dressed more for a night on the town than a day in the village. And she is in open pursuit of an eligible bachelor in the small community, making her a threat to both women and men as she flagrantly deploys her sexuality to achieve her amorous aims. Outsider Melanie Daniels is thus considered as much a threat to the safety of the community as are the birds.

Hitchcock himself provided no clear resolution to the film, leaving his audience to guess for themselves what it was that motivated the birds to turn on the outsider—and soon on insiders—with such violence. Refusing to allow the words "The End" to appear at the closing of the film, he simply closed the film with a scene of Miss Daniels being escorted to a car and driven back to whence she came—bloodied and bandaged from a savage attack of the birds—which remain on guard over the property she'd initially trespassed at the film's beginning. One is left wondering if the birds had singled out this blonde invader after all. Had she not been chased out of town by the birds, was it only a matter of time before the humans of the town gathered, circling and descending upon the interloper until she was driven out by Bodega Bay's own citizens?

Birds do indeed have a great deal to teach us about our own behavior. Perhaps the aggression of birds is no more evident, if not misread, than among the lowly chicken. Humans prey upon the chicken with such delight that it is our most commonly consumed flesh, and its image is emblazoned on everything from kitchen towels to crockery, making the witless bird virtually iconic as a symbol of home and hearth.

At the same time the symbol of the chicken conjures comfort, the living chicken is considered the most cowardly and unthinking of creatures. To be called "chicken" is a humiliation, a declaration that a person has no courage. But chickens are not exactly passive; they possess a pecking order and engage in social aggression so patterned and intentional that this fowl symbol of cowardice and ignorance might humble the keenest-eyed crow.

Poultry keepers have long known that chickens are anything but chicken. They are quite the bullies when opportunity, means and motive are before them. In any flock of chickens, there is a "top bird" who will dominate, and this top bird is almost always a male—unless there is no rooster available, in which case an old hen will be happy to rule the roost. The lower on the pecking order a chicken is, the more it is pecked at, bullied and pushed aside by higher-ranking chickens which will be the first to feed. And while the pecking order extends downward, should a dominate fowl fall sick or become wounded, its vulnerability marks it for attack by its stronger feathered friends.

Similarly, if a newcomer is introduced to the flock, a signal will be sounded by a dominant hen, and the newcomer will be pecked at and chased off by the flock. The aggression aimed at outsider birds is so common that poultry farmers learn to either segregate flocks, or introduce new ones slowly, keeping them penned but visible until the original flock has adjusted to the new blood. But even then there is no guarantee that the original flock will not attack the interlopers. Not every bird, it appears, is as free as a bird.

If birds be brutal, then what has it to do with us humans? The answer may be that of the ten to one hundred million species in the animal kingdom, birds, like humans, are among the rare species which will organize in groups to attack members of their own species. It is well known that intraspecies aggression, which is to say, aggression against at one's own kind, is widespread among all species when it comes to acts of *individuals* killing other individuals. But *collectively* organizing with others of the same species to eliminate a potential threat *from one's own kind* is exceedingly rare in the animal kingdom.

In other words, the key feature which distinguishes humans, birds, and chimpanzees (we'll get to those in a minute) from other members of the animal kingdom, at least regarding aggression, is organizing as a group to attack and destroy members of its own species. And when they do so, nearly every instance of intra-species aggression resembles a chicken fight—it is aimed at newcomers or individuals of any rank who have been weakened by sickness, age, injury, noticeable difference, or who have been singled out for harassment by a high-ranking member.

Which leads to the question, is it fair to say that there are bullies in the animal world? Research on a number of species demonstrates that individuals in the animal kingdom have differing levels of aggression, with some members more aggressive than others. But of interest to many researchers is not so much the anti-social behavior of individuals, *but how their aggression becomes contagious*, provoking the aggression of others.

And that means that if someone at the top of the hierarchy in your own human world is bullying you, you need to be aware of just how contagious that aggression can and will become. So let's take a look at how it works with other primates, the non-human kind.

Non-human Primates

Primate research has demonstrated the multitude of ways in which the bullying behavior of a high-status member can turn otherwise peaceful group members into a gang of thugs. Take rhesus monkeys, for example. In his book, *Macachiavellian Intelligence: How Rhesus Macaques and Humans Have Conquered the World*, primatologist Dario Maestripieri shows the cunning and manipulative strategies that rhesus monkeys deploy to gain status and power in their societies—in a manner which is strikingly similar to how humans behave at work and at war.

Maestripieri opens his book with the tale of a bully macaque who bites a well-liked adolescent male named Buddy. Rather than end the conflict by countering with an equally-painful blow, or showing submission and surrender to the bully, Buddy ran away in pain. By failing to gain or show respect, Buddy's display of weakness invited pursuit, and the bully escalated his abuse, as Buddy's friends rushed to join in the excitement. Rather than assist their friend who was under attack, however, Buddy's friends *pursued and attacked him*, causing the researchers who were observing the encounter to remove Buddy from the group for his own protection.

When Buddy was returned to the group, his former playmates badgered him, knocking him down and challenging him to fight. Still weak from the anesthesia the researchers had given him after removing him from the prior attack, Buddy's vulnerable state was exploited by the very playmates he grew up with. Mastripieri describes what happened:

> Buddy has spent every day of his life in the enclosure with all the other monkeys. They all eat the same food and sleep under the same roof. . . . . They were there when he was born. They held him and cuddled him when he was an infant. They have watched him grow, day by day, every day of his life. Yet, that day, if the researchers had not taken Buddy out of the group, he would have been killed. . . . He was weak and vulnerable. The behavior of the other monkeys changed swiftly and dramatically—from friendliness to intolerance, from play to aggression. Buddy's vulnerability became an opportunity for others to settle an old score, improve their position in the dominance hierarchy, or eliminate a potential rival for good. In rhesus macaque society, maintaining one's social status, being tolerated by others, and ultimately surviving at all may depend on how quickly one runs and how effectively one uses the right signal, with the right individual, at the right time (Mastripieri, 2007:4, 5).

This same pattern of harassment is found in wolves which will rarely organize to attack other packs of wolves, but will routinely single out weakened members of their own group for prolonged harassment, almost always instigated by an alpha wolf and carried out with the frenzied compliance of lower-ranking wolves. According to the renowned naturalist and wolf expert R. D. Lawrence, wolves literally "follow their leader" and turn on their pack members if a high-ranking alpha does so. To stop the harassment, the victimized wolf must show signs of submission—by lying on its back, exposing its throat, belly and groin to the alphas—*or by fleeing.*

But if this submission does not come soon enough, and flight is not possible or practical, even if the victimized wolf does eventually surrender and submit to its aggressors, the harassment may intensify. Like Buddy, the rhesus monkey who would have been killed had he remained with his playmates once his vulnerability was established, Lawrence noted a similar response from chronic aggression. A female wolf named Brigit was so harassed and shunned by her pack-mates over such a long time that she permanently embodied the signs of submission much as an abused spouse might do by walking with head lowered and eyes cast down in humility and fear.

Brigit moved in a semi-crouched position; her head and neck were carried low and her back legs were slightly bent, a posture that caused her spine to arch. Her tail was tucked between her thighs, almost pressing against the stomach, her ears were flattened backward, and her lips were parted in a solicitous grin. She studiously avoided eye contact and she whined constantly, but softly. In human terms Brigit would have appeared pathetic, but within the strictures of wolf hierarchy, her behavior advertised her total submission. Such voluntary and sustained subservience should have been sufficient to defuse the aggressive behavior of the Alphas, but for the fact that her continued presence within the pack contradicted the messages that her posture and manner were telegraphing.

For these reasons, [alpha wolves] Shawano and Denali continued to punish her (Lawrence, 1996:33).

Although she showed signs of submission, Brigit continued to be harassed because by the time she finally did submit, her role as victim had been too long established. By not leaving the pack once her new social role was fixed as a victim, she accepted her subordinate fate.

Perhaps Brigit feared leaving the pack because bad as it was among them, leaving the pack would make of her an intruder wherever she ventured. While leaving the group is essential for survival in the animal kingdom, once the group does attack, the quest to gain entry with another group may risk even greater aggression from the new group which is wary of outsiders. Once expelled, survival is precarious. And once an outsider, acceptance does not come readily, for animals as much as for humans.

We Ain't No Monkeys But We Know What We're Like

Perhaps the coordinated effort to harass, expel and kill one's own kind is best illustrated by a look at the ape world, from whence we came. When primatologist Jane Goodall first began her studies of chimpanzees in the wild in the early 1960's, she shared the prevailing belief that chimps are peaceful and playful rough-housing scamps. But after she witnessed the dominant females killing (and sometimes eating) the infants of subordinate females and brutally attacking each other, her views began to change. By 1970, after years of living and working with the clever and powerful primates, Goodall noted systematic warfare among organized bands of males against groups of rival males, leading to the conclusion that chimpanzees engage in warfare against their own species.

Warfare, of course, is distinct from mobbing behavior. Warfare is the organized aggression of one group against another group, whereas mobbing is the organized aggression of a group against an individual. But Goodall's findings are significant because they stimulated debates on the nature of human aggression. If there is an evolutionary origin to human aggression against our own kind, does that then justify it?

That's where culture comes in. Culture is what humans have cooked up to regulate our instincts. Take, for example, sex. Sex is an instinct, but sex among close family members leads to all sorts of problems, from increasing genetic abnormalities within population groups, to increasing tensions, conflicts and rivalries within the family, not to mention messing family members up something awful. For that reason, all cultures have some form of an incest taboo. Who is included in that taboo may vary (though mother and child incest is universally prohibited), but all cultures have one. Cultures also have different rules for who can marry whom, and what happens if you transgress with the wrong kind of person. In order to regulate the human instinct for sex, cultures have created rules for who we can have it with.

Similarly with the human instinct of aggression. Cultures establish codes of conduct to maintain cohesion and stability among its members, and hence a number of our cultural rules, codes and laws pertain to forms of human aggression. The flip side of human aggression is human cooperation. Who we cooperate with and why, and who we enter into conflict with and why, is never random. It is always strategic.

We are not alone in that regard. Evolutionary biologist Dario Maestripieri draws on primate research to show the strategic social cunning which rhesus monkeys will engage in to negotiate conflict and cooperation toward individual reward. For the rhesus monkey, individual status and fortune are the goal for which others are befriended, sabotaged or shunned.

> In rhesus macaque society, maintaining one's social status, being tolerated by others, and ultimately surviving at all may depend on how quickly one runs and how effectively one uses the right signal, with the right individual, at the right time. A rhesus macaque can wake up one morning, feel a little drowsy, and find himself in danger of being killed by his best friends (Maestripieri 2007:4).

In other words, where chimpanzees are warriors, rhesus macaques, like humans, are politicians at work and at play. Less intelligent than chimps, *who* a rhesus monkey knows is more important to survival than *what* they know, and attaining and maintaining the protection of high-ranking macaques is necessary for survival.

Macaques instinctively understand the survival benefits of strategic alliances, and for this reason, new immigrant males will subordinate themselves to senior males and females. In times of conflict, however, these subordinate males will turn on other subordinates and refuse to help them when they are in trouble, assisting the aggressors, not the victims. In this way, newcomers who are otherwise vulnerable and powerless, can achieve status by joining in the aggression against other newcomers or against subordinates who are perceived as a threat by the dominant members of the group.

Biology again plays a crucial role in primate survival. For macaques, the most important relationships involve close kin; although they will attack other monkeys they are biologically related to, they are far more likely to assist and cooperate with kin than they are to hurt them. But in the world of non-kin, according to Maestripieri, macaques forge relationships with other macaques if they fall within one of three categories: those they can have sex with, those they can do business with, and those they can victimize. (If this sounds a lot like the place you work at, at least now you know it's a primate thing.)

While infants are the most likely to be victimized among macaque society, any macaque who is weakened, vulnerable, or a threat to one's social relationships is a target for attack. And it is not only males who are the aggressors—females are extremely aggressive, even when there is no infant or sexual rivalry involved. Although macaque society is organized around females, with daughters remaining with their mothers and sons migrating to find mates in other groups after they mature, males remain the most powerful members of macaque society because they are needed for protection.

Female macaques are thus subordinate to males, but they gain status when a new female attempts to enter the group, which provides them the opportunity to dominate the newcomer. This pattern is also reflected in humans, as subordinate members respond to the entry of newcomers, and females readily turn on other females who join the group, particularly when the subordination of females is marked, or there are few females within the group.

Maestripieri notes how eagerly rhesus females will gang up on other females:

> The lowest-ranking females in the group, in fact, will be the individuals who immediately attack the newcomer and who continue to harass her for days, or weeks, or months, long after everybody else has gotten tired of it. This is because they finally have somebody they can dominate and finally get the chance to express all of their aggression and frustration they have repressed in a life spent at the bottom of the hierarchy. A female newcomer also gives the lowest-ranking females the chance to form coalitions with higher-ranking individuals and redirect aggression and, finally, the chance to have a scapegoat of their own. Introducing a new female into a group of rhesus macaques is a bad idea and shouldn't be done, but it's the best thing that could ever happen to the lowest-ranking females in the group(Maestripieri 2007:87).

In sum, nothing is more guaranteed to convert the hyper-competitive macaques into cooperative team-players than the entry of a newcomer. Because newcomers rarely migrate alone, and are almost always followed by more of their kind, the arrival of a newcomer sounds the alarm for the group to unite and prepare for war, and it is the subordinates—rather than the bullying leaders—of the group that will prove to be the fighting force defending the group.

The rhesus monkey leaders are protected by their subordinates in two important respects. The subordinates prove to be effective fighters by releasing their pent-up aggression at the newcomers. By sacrificing their own lives and limbs, they also protect their leaders from getting killed or attacked themselves. They may lose a bit of blood or flesh, but they gain the approval and respect of their leaders. Leaders are willing to risk losing an occasional subordinate to serious injury or death, but they are not willing to sacrifice all their subordinates because they need them to do battle against one's enemies. Or, as Sun Tzu, the author of the classic, *The Art of War*, put it sometime around 500 B.C., "Regard your soldiers as your beloved children and they will follow you into the deepest valleys. Look on them as your sons and they will die with you." Which is to say, when a battle is ignited, leaders will bend over backwards to love and protect their subordinates. Remember that.

Whether due to the arrival of newcomers whose strength and power must be tested, or due to the potential for a subordinate group to overthrow a dominant group, conflict is most lethal when threats to power are at stake. Once power has been established, conflicts typically end with a few cuts and bruises and the surrender of the least powerful monkey. But the more precarious dominant/subordinate relationships become and the more change is introduced to a rhesus society, the more members are scrutinized *for any sign of challenging behaviors*. Those who adjust their behavior and submit to the ruling power, Maestripieri points out, are the ones who are most likely to survive, while those who are unwilling to show submission and surrender to their masters are more likely to be killed. And the time such aggression is most likely to transpire, is when something is shaking up their hierarchy. The same thing happens in organizations—whenever hierarchies are changing, there will be challenges to—and quests for—power. Consequently, any sign of challenging behavior can lead to swift retribution—not just from those in power, but from those seeking it, as well as those fearing it.

How do rhesus monkeys minimize their costs when seeking power? By forming coalitions. Rhesus monkeys are strategic in who they look to for assistance, selectively gazing upon subordinates whose loyalties they test in times of trouble. As these coalitions are formed, the victim also tries to solicit help, but in a far more desperate manner.

When victims of aggression ask for help from others, they use the same behaviors as the aggressors, but with a lot more screaming. They probably scream from fear or pain, but with their screaming they accomplish two goals: they disorient the aggressor, thereby interrupting the aggression, and they attract the attention of other individuals and solicit their support. . . . Whether or not the message reaches its intended recipient, whether or not it's properly decoded, and more importantly, whether or not the intended recipient gives a damn about it, depends on who the transmitter is, who they are fighting against, and who else is watching and listening (Maestripieri 2007:49,50).

Applying these behaviors to humans might explain why it is that people who "complain" about discrimination or mistreatment might appear increasingly unstable over time. As the threats against them increase, they scream louder, in hopes it will solicit support from others, and bring intervention from leadership to stop the mistreatment. But rhesus monkeys may have another lesson to teach us about how leaders perceive these screams:

You might expect that everyone would ask for help from the king and the queen of their group, but that's not always a good idea, for a couple of reasons. First, like all royals, the rhesus king and queen are very good at feigning indifference when the requests for help come from somebody at the bottom of their society. Second, if they are really bothered by all the noise and insulted by being asked to get their hands dirty with fighting, they may intervene and attack the victim who's seeking help and not the aggressor (Maestripieri 2007:50).

In other words, humans might consider what happens to a primate when it runs to its rulers for protection. The monkey-business of work is indeed, monkey business.

Biologist Debra Niehoff has studied how animal behavior helps us to understand the social and biological foundations of human aggression. She has noted that studies of aggression tend to focus on individuals. But because aggression involves multiple individuals, she suggests that studying group behavior may tell us something about how aggression escalates when participants respond to the behavior of others.

> For solitary species (e.g. the mouse), aggression is a solution to the problem of keeping others away. But for highly social species like primates (including humans), aggression is one solution to the challenges of group living. For these species, aggression is a tool that group members can use to define complex social relationships, a behavioral probe that periodically tests the reactions of others and adjusts the tenor of future encounters accordingly, a mechanism that paradoxically promotes cohesion rather than dispersion. As a result of this new recognition that aggressive behavior is a two-way street, today's behavioral researchers stress the importance of studying aggression—whether in the lab or in the field—*from a social perspective that includes the victim as well as the aggressor and bystanders as well as participants.* (Niehoff 1998:56, emphasis added).

If Niehoff is correct in looking to group behavior to understand aggression, then the current literature on bullies in the workplace—which focus on individual bullies—may be off the mark by not looking more closely to how these "bullies" enlist the support of others to harass a targeted "victim."

But another, far more uncomfortable, conclusion follows this logic. If "bullying" is a group process, contrary to prevailing accounts of workplace bullying as having nothing to do with anything the "victim" does, there must be behavioral features that harassed individuals exhibit that merit reflection. Think back to those rhesus monkeys who failed to submit or those birds who didn't fly off—they may have done nothing "wrong," but they failed to act in a manner to ensure their survival once they became the target of aggression. Which gets us back to rats.

For all the talk of our similarity to monkeys and apes, it's the brains of rats that scientists most often poke and prod to learn about human brains; for better or worse, the human brain is strikingly similar to the brain of a rat. And perhaps our behaviors are much the same—whether living the rat race, feeling like a cornered rat, ratting on someone or smelling a rat, when we speak of rats, we tend to also think of humans—badly behaving humans.

Scientists who study aggression have looked to rat behavior for clues to how humans will behave under certain circumstances or stressors. And what they have found is that the aggressive behaviors of rats are not isolated and random. Instead, rat aggression reflects a characteristic sequence and pattern, with sporadic bursts of aggression followed by intervals of calm and isolation. Aggression in humans is much the same. When humans become aggressive, our aggression is most likely to occur intermittently, as with the abusive spouse who alternates between violent outbursts and loving attention.

In her study of aggression, Niehoff has noted that this intermittent pattern of attack among rats is accompanied by similarly patterned behaviors on the part of the rats who are on the receiving end of the attacks. "The intertwined dance of alpha and intruder reveals the social complexity of the aggressive encounter. Each action on the part of one member of the pair elicits an equal and opposite reaction from the other." (Niehoff 1998:66). To understand these responses to aggression, it is useful to understand how fear affects behavior and the brain.

After repeated stress from electrical shocks, rats adopt defensive behaviors that initially cause them to retreat and avoid the pain-inducing stimulant. Over time they may appear to return to normalcy, but if shocked again, however slightly, they immediately return to the heightened state of fear as if the shock were as severe as before.

In other words, once a rat has been repeatedly shocked, it may recover enough to interact as before, but the memory of the shock has not gone away. The slightest reminder that it could return and the rat will respond as if hit with the full force of the original stimulant, and the fear-circuit is reactivated. As the old saying goes, if a cat is attacked by a snake, it will fear even a rope. Fear, it seems, is remarkably similar across species, and understanding how it operates helps us to understand how targets respond to the repeated attacks of a workplace mobbing.

> Fear conditioning occurs in fruit flies, snails, and reptiles, as well as in rats and humans. . . Easily elicited and readily related to naturally occurring behavior in a threatening situation, fear conditioning has been the foundation for significant advances in our understanding of how the brain translates events in the outside world into emotional memories of long-standing and profound significance." (Niehoff 1998:69,70).

What might fear conditioning among rats mean for workers in the rat race? It means that mobbing is, indeed, "crazy making." Once mobbing commences, "paranoia" may well be a normal response that turns healthy workers into frightened, skittish people who interpret the benign behavior of other workers as threatening, and whose emotional responses may appear to others to be abnormal, when, in fact, they are perfectly normal and adaptive responses to having been subjected to repeated abuse.

So how do rats adjust to chronic abuse? Niehoff discusses the behavior of alpha males who assert their authority by thrashing invader males and singling out subordinate males for excessive abuse. The male most likely to attempt an overthrow of the alpha rat is the one most vulnerable to being targeted, suggesting that it is not the most passive, least threatening of the species who is necessarily the most likely to be abused, but it may well be the stronger, more clever rat who must, quite literally in the rat world, watch his back.

Like rhesus monkeys, chickens and wolves, rats have hierarchies, and any challenge to this hierarchy, such as a lowly rat attempting to push aside a more powerful rat for a bigger bite of the cheese, results in swift and fierce aggression.

But unlike wolves, who tend to accept their lowly position with the grace of a well-trained servant, rats find the limited options and violent encounters of their subordinate lives very stressful.

> As a result of this harshly imposed hierarchy, subordinates lead lives of tremendous anxiety. Over time, they lose weight, sleep less, avoid the colony females, and become increasingly defensive. Ultimately, they die sooner—not directly, from battle wounds, but gradually, presumably from the exhausting toll imposed by chronic stress (Niehoff 1998:70).

Just as rats waste away when repeatedly attacked, so, too, do humans. It is little wonder that targets of workplace aggression report weight loss, headaches, hypertension, heart disease, cancers and other illnesses during and following chronic aggression, making them less productive and effective at their work, and thereby appearing less valuable to the workplace.

But not all rats are created equal. Just as some humans can be subjected to chronic stress and not exhibit symptoms of Post-Traumatic Stress Disorder (PTSD), so, too, do some rats endure chronic abuse with few of the expected signs and symptoms that most rats exhibit. Some might find these exceptions to the norm to be an example of "survival of the fittest," that is, chronic abuse is viewed as a ritual that tests a worker's endurance, similar to a rite of passage that initiates must master before being granted admission to an exclusive group.

Yet this "survival of the fittest" defense for abuse is unconvincing. It is just as possible that those people who do withstand chronic torment with little or no visible scars are not necessarily "stronger" and "better" workers, or even saintly masters of the human soul who can pass through battlefields, raging fires and even shopping malls on Christmas Eve, without so much as even flinching. They might instead be potential "alphas" whose emotional resilience reflects an emotional void, which may be a marker of their own aggressive tendencies which will eventually—in the right context—manifest in aggression toward others. In other words, those who aren't scarred by chronic abuse might not be "the fittest," as much as "the coldest."

Not only is aggression in rats a way to maintain social hierarchies by lashing out at insubordinate subordinates who challenge the alphas, rats, just as wolves and monkeys, are more likely to act aggressively when they cannot flee. Rats who are held captive in mazes not only suffer from the chronic stress of trying to get out of the maddening maze they've been placed in, but they are also more likely to turn vicious and attack each other when trapped in a maze, than if left in the wild or in more open spaces. Research on rats has found that when placed in a maze and offered a means to escape—only to receive an electrical shock each time they tried to do so—rats either crouched and froze in terror, jumping in fear at the slightest noise, or they ran wildly about in a state of panic.

Similarly, workers who are punished repeatedly learn to freeze in their tracks or run around like Chicken Little screaming the sky is crashing down on them. If they freeze or "lay low," they fall silent to workplace abuses, do not strive to be more productive (and hence competitive), and become as invisible as possible. And if they panic, they will turn to everyone they can for help, taking any action they think might stop the abuse from escalating. And we've already seen what good that does, just ask our screaming monkeys.

But what happens when the abuse is both long-lasting and aimed at *all* the subordinates? Is their shared suffering likely to unite them? In a study of rats trapped in a maze and subjected to repeated shocks over a long period of time, the pattern of freezing or panicking changed. After six weeks of such abuse, 25 of the original thirty rats who were shocked every time they tried to escape the maze had killed *each other*. Fear and anxiety, among rats at least, does more than paralyze a rat's responses or send them scurrying around in a crazy state of panic. When placed in a continual state of fear and anxiety, even good rats go bad and resort to lethal violence *against each other.*

What could these findings tell us about how humans behave in the workplace when they feel powerless to escape the maze of institutional dead ends and false hopes, or when a tight job market limits their ability to quit and move on (and raises the risk for the worker who faces being fired)? Does fear and anxiety among humans increase the potential for violence in the workplace in the same way it does with rats? According to Niehoff (1998:73), it does. "Whether sparked by electricity, drugs, or an experimenter's hand," she writes, "these models reflect a condition that, like the violence that triggers it, is the cumulative result of a dynamic interaction between the traumatized brain and a provocative environment."

In other words, being subjected to constant fear and anxiety changes the brain. It changes the way rats—and humans—interpret and respond to social cues, and experience the world in which they live. But to a manager seeking to be rid of an employee, this finding is nothing new; the calculating manager counts on rats being rats.

"How do you force people who work for you to be loyal to you, only to you, and not develop some sniveling affection for one another?" asks Fortune Magazine columnist Stanley Bing in his best-selling book, *What Would Machievelli Do? The Ends Justify the Meanness.* His answer? "You set them at one another. And watch them rip out one another's throats in an effort to please you better."

The calculating manager also understands that once the battle for power has begun, there's only one outcome. As Freddy Krueger said, "There's only one cure for me, buddy boy, you got to die!"

Death is Not the End

While aggression among animals, as among people, often continues until someone dies or leaves the group, society lives on. If a harassed animal lives, but is forced to migrate to another group, the animal continues to suffer as it struggles to survive in isolation, and find a new group to accept it (as a vulnerable newcomer).

As for the group that harassed and exiled the animal, there will be a peaceful period—but not one without anxiety. Having witnessed the harassment of one of their own kind, and in many cases having participated in it, subordinate animals will adjust to the changed status and social roles that the battle produced, creating new dominant/subordinate relationships—as well as new conflicts. Because one of the reasons a dominant animal openly abuses a subordinate is to display its power, the exodus (or death) of a harassed animal sends a message to all animals that the same fate awaits them if they irritate the alphas.

Whether they are chimpanzees, wolves, rats or rhesus monkeys, challenging the status of another member of the group invites severe harassment. Whenever power is at stake, the stakes are high, and the fight will be to the finish.

Yet other factors contribute to an animal being harassed, and they appear to be the same across species. In addition to challenges to power, any animal that is weakened by injury, sickness or old age is vulnerable to abuse, and any animal that is openly abused by an alpha will find that its playmates and even kin will not come to its aid, but will instead join the alphas in tormenting the wounded animal. This process of harassment begins early, with subtle cues that the dominant members display, such as ignoring or not sharing with certain subordinates, forcing a subordinate to show signs of submission, and even the more blatant "show looking" of alpha macaques who look to specific subordinates to see if they will or will not join in a battle.

How does this primate behavior look in the workplace? Stanley Bing has an answer:

> Invite select associates to some meetings, while excluding others. Do not be consistent. Create a continuous sense of uncertainty in people around you about whether they are in or out. . . Talk

about others to their peers. Sometimes you can compliment them, sometimes you can bitch about them. Create the feeling in all people that you're willing to talk about them behind their backs, and pretty candidly, too. Be very clear in discussions that someone else's priority has effectively killed those of their peers. . . what you want is an atmosphere of high-energy, cutthroat rivalry among those who surround you. This focuses all activity in the neighborhood on your approval. All action, no matter how smart or lucrative, is valued only if it meets with your strong approval and places the actor one notch up on his associates (Bing: 2002:97, 98).

And who gets attacked? Think again about animals. Two things in particular stand out as "risk factors" for harassment in the animal world. The first is that a newcomer will be viewed as a threat. Newcomers face three choices: to assimilate through submission; to overpower the dominant alphas by winning a battle (which is rare, because the dominant members will have formed coalitions); or be driven out through death or exile. *Difference* is the key risk factor here, as fear of the unknown leads animals, just as it does with humans, to group together in defense against any potential threat the unknown entity might pose.

The second factor that puts an animal at risk for collective harassment is finding itself in a confined area. When there is no means of escape, such as when an animal is held in captivity, stuck in a maze, or its territory has been cut off, all members of the group will be more prone to aggression, and when the aggression commences, it will be more severe than if the animal could freely depart.

Thus among animals, it is newcomers, those who are different, those who are weakened and vulnerable, and those who are in a confined area, who are most vulnerable to group aggression. And just what a confined area means in the human world, is something we'll get to in Chapter Two. It's not necessarily a jail cell.

Experiments in Human Aggression

So what does all this stuff about birds and monkeys have to do with how our coworkers and others behave? After all, animals do not have the minds of humans and cannot control their nature like humans can. Or might we be overestimating the capacity of humans to control ourselves? The truth is, we humans do have trouble with controlling our primal behaviors, particularly when the rest of the group is out of control. As a few famous psychology experiments have demonstrated time and time again, if given the opportunity to behave like animals, we most certainly will.

In 1971, psychologist Philip Zimbardo conducted the Stanford Prison experiments, where research subjects were assigned roles as prison guards or prisoners. Zimbardo found that when playing the role of guards, ordinary non-sadistic people became increasingly aggressive, were arbitrary in their punishments, and exhibited pleasure at the humiliation of their "prisoners." The more they dehumanized the prisoners, acted under the cloak of anonymity, and realized there would be no accountability for their abuses, the more their aggression escalated.

Even among those guards who initially resisted the aggression, *all* eventually rationalized their decision to join ranks with authoritarian guards, and all soon rationalized their behavior as legitimate due to the behavior of the one being punished—even when the one being punished had clearly done nothing wrong and the punishment was by any standard a violation of human decency.

As for the prisoners? They didn't fare much better. Zimbardo's team found that the arbitrariness of the punishments the guards inflicted, the lack of privacy, public humiliation, and increasing powerlessness led those playing the role of "prisoner" to become enraged, confused and ultimately defeated.

Perhaps most disturbing of all, no matter how great and arbitrary the cruelty became, none of those who inflicted the brutality expressed any remorse when they returned home and were free of the artificial "prison" in which they'd acted with impunity. By having legitimated their actions as necessary and brought on by the target, the "guards" had come to believe they acted morally and appropriately.

In a similar experiment conducted in 1963, social psychologist Stanley Milgram instructed his research subjects to administer what they (falsely) believed to be electric shocks on unsuspecting "learners" who gave the wrong answers to test questions. Unbeknownst to the research subjects, the "learners" were actors whose faces were not seen (they were behind an opaque screen), but whose feigned screams could be heard. As their screams commenced and the ones inflicting the "shocks" expressed concern about what they were doing, they were assured by researchers (wearing white lab coats to connote authority) not to worry about it and to increase the voltage. Surprisingly, *almost all did so*—in many cases beyond what would have been lethal levels had the shocks been real.

These experiments demonstrated that ordinary humans are very susceptible to authority and conformity, and that many can easily become sadistic under certain conditions. These experiments have also shown that if permitted to inflict pain by someone in a position of authority, *and not held accountable* for the consequences of their actions, humans will not only inflict pain on others, but they will continue to do so above and beyond what is necessary to satisfy the authority figures—and they will not stop until they are made to do so. Moreover, the participants in both experiments showed little remorse for their aggression. Regardless of how they'd behaved, they believed they were doing "the right thing," and "had no choice."

Zimbardo's experiment, replicated in multiple variations over the decades since it was initially conducted, was used to explain why soldiers who tortured inmates at Abu Ghraib were not aberrant "bad apples," as the military depicted them, but ordinary non-pathological people who had been put into an organizational context that rewarded them for cruel behavior.

So what about the people you work or live with? Mobbing doesn't involve strangers hiding behind a partition as in Milgram's experiments, or prisoners who have ostensibly violated social laws as Zimbardo's subjects represented. Mobbing is instead real people acting with increasing aggression against people they know and in many cases once liked and admired.

But friendship has its limits, as elementary school teacher Jane Elliott demonstrated in 1968 when she divided her third-grade classroom into "blue eyed" and "brown eyed" students. In the aftermath of the assassination of Martin Luther King, Jr., Ms. Elliott set out to test how "difference" is learned. After dividing her students by eye color, she told them that one eye color was superior to another, and that those with a certain eye color were bad, stupid, lazy and deserving of shunning and abuse.

To be sure eye color was noticeable from afar, she had the target group wear paper colors around their neck—and watched in horror as her students almost immediately began to act abhorrently to their collared friends and classmates. Moreover, their abuse grew particularly aggressive at recess—when she, the authority figure, was no longer present. And just as Zimbardo found that the "prisoners" in his experiments had internalized their roles and accepted their fates, Ms. Elliott found the persecuted children began to believe the claims made against them, withdraw almost immediately and perform poorly in school. Ms. Elliott has since replicated her experiment over the last half century in a variety of social settings, from schools to workplaces to prisons, *and the results have never changed.*

What these experiments in human aggression have shown us, and what animal experiments have demonstrated, is that when told by someone in authority to turn on their friends, people (and monkeys) will do so.

Which brings us now to mobbing.

CHAPTER 2

Organizational Cultures

Now that you have an idea of how animals act toward each other, you are probably getting a better idea of how humans act toward each other. It's when humans behave in a group that you can expect our animal nature to come out. But there's another factor that will shape how that behavior is manifest, and that's the environmental context, which is to say, the organizational culture in which the group functions.

By considering the organizational cultures that we live and work in, we can better understand the roles that people play inside them. How power is distributed, how hierarchies are structured, and how resources are distributed and accessed, all influence how people will interact with each other, particularly during times of stress or conflict.

Unfortunately, much of what we read about bullying and organizational cultures comes down to "healthy" and "unhealthy" workplaces, or "ethical" leadership compared to "unethical" leadership. With this line of thinking, it is assumed that whether or not abuse will be tolerated is dependent on how good or bad the place and its leadership are.

There is certainly a great deal to be said about leadership and its role in fostering cooperative workplace environments. Indeed, the integrity of leadership—or lack of it—cannot be understated in predicting how things will turn out once a workplace conflict is ignited. But if you assume that moral or amoral leadership is all there is to it, you risk misreading the cues of how your own actions or words might be interpreted by others in that organization. Keep in mind that those nasty monkeys and birds and wolves that tormented the vulnerable among them, were not necessarily "bad" monkeys or birds or wolves. Most of the time they were just, well, animals.

Applying the findings in animal studies to the human world, it becomes apparent which settings are most prone to the worst aggression. As we've seen from the rats in the maze in Chapter One, being cornered and unable to escape a stressful environment increases the chances that animals will become aggressive.

Any job where people cannot easily leave—or be expelled—is ripe for aggression. Any job where there is increased job security through union membership, a tenure system, or military service is ripe for mobbing because the worker cannot easily be fired, and is unlikely to quit easily. Professions that require a great deal of training, but with limited job opportunities, such as academic tenure-track positions, are particularly prone to group aggression because people will not give them up easily—they will stay for the fight. Airline pilots and air traffic controllers, clergy, people in the entertainment industry and other professions where people cannot easily apply their skills elsewhere may be among the most vulnerable to collective attacks. And federal workers, such as postal employees, whose educational background may be relatively limited, but who earn a comfortable living, are not likely to readily leave their jobs (thus relinquishing longevity and benefits) if they are being harassed. The military is a classic example of a profession where the members cannot leave of their own free will, and where mobbing (along with sexual and physical assault) is exceptionally high. People close to retirement who cannot easily find work at their age and who will lose all or part of their retirement benefits will not readily leave. And during a harsh economy where losing a job can be economically and psychologically devastating, any workplace can become a form of captivity that breeds primal aggression in every worker—no matter how good or ethical its leadership.

Another factor that increases aggression among animals is limited resources. The same is true in the human world; **in organizational settings where there is insufficient support or the necessary resources to succeed, there will be increased aggression.** Where you find raises only given to the top five or ten percent, or where budget cuts or mergers are slashing positions, salaries and perks, you will find heightened competition and aggression. Thus, any organization may find itself prone to aggression during turbulent economic times.

Similarly, we've seen in the animal world that abuse escalates when something comes along to destabilize the leadership, such as an alpha intruder, the sickness or death of a leader, or an environmental crisis. In the human world **any institutional change that destabilizes the leadership will increase the risk of aggression within the organization, no matter how good or bad its members.**

The significance to hierarchies in maintaining order is not only apparent in times of changing leadership, but **the more limited the opportunities for advancement in any organizational hierarchy, the greater the propensity for aggression.**

For example, in professions such as nursing or teaching, employees are usually able to find similar work elsewhere if they lose their jobs, even in bad economic times. Yet two features of these professions make them particularly ripe for workplace aggression. The first is that there are few opportunities for advancement. So there is not only greater competition among the workforce for the few promotions that become available, but when someone does attain a management position, they don't want to jeopardize that place in the institutional power structure. If that is the case, any sign of insubordination or conflict among subordinates can be perceived as a threat to that leadership, and swift and aggressive action to punish the perceived threat will ensue—even if that perceived threat is nothing more than a teacher questioning a policy or reporting a workplace problem—a problem the principal might not want to take blame for should it happen on his or her watch.

A second feature of the teaching and nursing professions is they disproportionately employ a single gender. **Wherever diversity in any respect is limited, anyone who does not fit the image of the majority will stand out as "different," and hence, be vulnerable for a longer period to newcomer status.** We have already seen what that means for animals, and for humans it is no different. Those who look different are perceived as a threat; it's an evolutionary thing. That doesn't mean it is right, it just explains why difference can lead to primal behavior, which is to say, brutish and nasty conduct.

When the gender in an organization is predominantly female or male, competition will be high. Males tend to be raised to be competitive for status, resources and mates. Females are also raised to compete with each other, but much of that competition centers on achieving male attention—as an indirect route to status and resources. And while much has changed in terms of gender, and women are aiming for a whole lot more in life than a protective mate, the enculturation of competition within genders, whether male or female, is high.

What this means to someone in the workplace is that **if there is primarily one gender dominating the workforce, not only will aggression be greater *within* that gender, but anyone not of that gender will be noticeably different.** Thus in both teaching and nursing, mobbing is common in two ways: as women turn on women, and as men enter the workforce. When men join a predominantly female profession, they are vulnerable to attack—an attack that unites the otherwise competitive female gender. (The same dynamic is prevalent in occupations that are primarily male, such as construction or the military. As women join their ranks, they become newcomers marked for attack, which will prevail at least until there is greater gender equity, and as long as leadership permits it.)

Another characteristic of organizations that are prone to mobbing is where professional identity is visibly displayed and a source of great pride. In occupations where people wear uniforms and marks of their achievements, such as badges, medals, or stripes, the importance of belonging and the honor of advancement are emphasized and visible. Professions where people are addressed by honorific titles are similarly characterized by pride in one's identity. Mobbing strips away that identity, and thus when it occurs, it progresses rapidly because those around the mobbing target will close ranks without hesitation and seek to strip the target of that shared identity. Moreover, to lose one's identity and right to an honorific title or uniform or other marker of achievement and respect, is particularly damaging. It strips a person not just of their identity, but their social history and achievements.

In a nutshell this means that professions with few alphas, rigid hierarchies, limited diversity or few chances for advancement are ripe for mobbing, as are professions or occupations where the opportunities for leaving and finding something comparable are limited. **Understanding these structural distinctions does far more to predict how a workplace conflict will unfold than does distinguishing "good" organizations from "bad" ones**.

The significance of organizational structure to human behavior was a lesson I learned from a student. I was teaching a course on the anthropology of warfare, when the issue of "embedded anthropologists" in war zones became a topic of national discussion. The U.S. military had begun recruiting anthropologists to help teach combatants about cultural differences in order to avoid unnecessary hostilities. Proponents of the practice argued that occupying forces could be more effective if they better understood the culture in which they were fighting and could potentially reduce hostilities that cultural misunderstandings provoked. Opponents argued that anthropologists have an ethical obligation to protect the people with whom they work and study. Using information about a culture in order to educate soldiers to more effectively combat or conquer them has been an issue of great concern to the anthropology profession.

As I lectured in class about the different views to this argument, and elaborated on the importance of understanding cultural differences, a student interjected. He was a combat veteran, and had told me that he had fought in over one hundred clandestine operations in the course of his career.

"It doesn't matter where I've fought or when I've fought," he told the class, "the cultural differences never mattered. Wherever I was there were the same four or five guys, and that's who we needed to defeat."

I stared blankly, curious as to where he was going with his "same four or five guys" thing.

"In every country I've ever fought in, no matter how small-scale and primitive the forces were or how large-scale and high tech, there is always a warlord, a couple of guards protecting him, and one or two jackals waiting in the shadows for an opportunity to seize power—and you never know who the jackals are; sometimes they're real good at hiding their ambitions. But the most dangerous of all," he said, "is the Worried Killer. Watch out for the Worried Killer, because he'll kill you over nothing and not even care."

This description sounded, at first, rather like a made-for-TV-movie script, if not my own department. I was dubious, but he elaborated. He explained that the warlord may or may not be intelligent, cunning or even respected by his people. But he will not tolerate any threat to his power, and he will surround himself with a couple of people whose job it is to protect him from scandal or defeat. Anyone wanting to attack the warlord has to first identify and go after his guards.

The jackals, he explained, are tricksters. Some are obvious, in which case they can be easily controlled. But very often there is someone nearby who is watching for any sign of instability, and when the opportunity comes, they'll seize it. The jackals, he explained, succeed by keeping their ambitions concealed. To identify the jackals, it is not enough to spot the obvious suck-ups and social climbers. It is also critical to assume that *anyone* could be a jackal.

Which reminds me of something I read in the *Chronicle of Higher Education* a few years back about surviving the tenure track. The author shared this bit of advice he'd once been told: "Remember that every department has at least one ax murderer, but you won't know in advance who it is so you'd better be on your guard."

In other words, a jackal.

"But what's the Worried Killer?" I asked my student, "And what makes him so dangerous?"

These other guys, he explained, are by their nature psychopaths. But the Worried Killer wasn't born a psychopath. He may have achieved his position by birth or accident or opportunity, but along the way he has had to do some things he doesn't like. He's been bullied and abused by everyone above him, and forced to bully and abuse people beneath him in order to please those above him. After awhile he hates himself for some of the things he's done, so he focuses his rage on those beneath him. He knows he can be kicked downward at any moment so the slightest challenge someone poses is perceived by him as a serious threat. He'll eliminate that threat as fast and permanently as he can and be happy doing it—not because he's sadistic, but because it's spared him from being punished.

Hmmm, I thought. Now there was a concept worth considering. I wasn't sure how useful it was in warfare, but it sure made sense in organizational settings. All too often organizational "leadership" is discussed as if it's something unified, a homogenous group of like-minded people who are ethical or not ethical, good or bad, humane or inhumane. Rarely are the fissures among that leadership considered when contemplating how a conflict within that institution will be handled.

Consider the issue of bullying. In books and blogs on bullying, "the bully" might be a boss, or a coworker. But in any case, the focus is on the bad guy to be eliminated, with HR (Human Resources) widely known to be the last place one should go to report bullying. HR does not represent the interests of employees. HR represents the employers—management.

So HR is not going to tell management how to behave. What management wants, management gets. But "management" is not exactly one big happy family. So who does the common worker report a workplace problem to?

Consider the Worried Killer. In an organizational context, the "Worried Killer" is likely to be the person in a precarious position of power—the unit or department heads who are frequently rotated, or the vice-this or assistant-that—the one's just beneath the big guys. That does not mean that every department or unit head is going to be a Worried Killer. What it means is that before taking a problem to this level of management, you should ask yourself certain questions.

How long have they been in that position? How secure is it? How are they evaluated? Who above them supported their ascension? Who above them has worked with them in another capacity—either the prior department or unit head, as a coworker, or in some other capacity? That person may well be the one a "Worried Killer" reports to—what is this person's reputation? Don't think in terms of how well liked and admired they are, but how swiftly they are known to deal with a problem, and how rapidly they are climbing to the top—that will give you an idea of how they will respond to the problem.

Consider how they have responded to conflicts in the past. Do they prefer to avoid conflict? If so, beware of bringing them a conflict to deal with. Do they work things out informally and fairly, without turning them into something bigger? If so, you may well be safe asking for their help; but do so cautiously.

Consider other questions. Do they discuss issues openly or are they prone to closed door discussions? Even if they regularly come to you for your input on an issue, if it's behind closed doors or in some other discreet manner, they will do the same with others. What that means for you is if you bring them a problem, they will be conferring with others about what they think—which may well bode ill for you.

How do they handle evaluations? Do they punish and reward? If so, be prepared to be punished if you bring them a problem—and for others to be rewarded if they eliminate the problem.

In sum, low-level managers who are receiving a significant monetary or professional reward for their work, but are in a position that frequently rotates, and who have a prior relationship with someone above them in leadership, may very well be "Worried Killers." If they have a history of punishing some and rewarding others based on perceived slights or anything other than merit, be on guard. If they are bullying you, reporting it to someone above them is likely to be futile, because they have put that person in that position for a reason. Do not kid yourself that they do not recognize what kind of person they have put there.

If someone else is the problem, do not bring the problem to the Worried Killer, unless you have no other option (and you almost always do have another option). They will not want anyone above them finding out there is a problem on their watch. Instead, the problem they may very well bring to those above them is not the problem you reported. The problem they bring to the attention of their higher-ups will be—you.

"There's nothing management hates more than the corporate office looking into a problem with one employee," Phil Porter writes in *Eat or Be Eaten*, "When they do, the employee is added to the 'kill-at-all costs' list. Every member of management will conspire to snag him, even if it does take a while."

Finally, whatever you do, **do not assume that your manager's—or anybody's—political or religious views, or any stated values, will affect how they respond to the conflict**. This is so important it can't be repeated enough, and it applies to everyone in the organization. People will respond to a conflict based on their self-interest, which almost always ends up to be what would please those above them—not below or alongside them. After they've acted they will justify their actions as first, *necessary*, and second, *the only thing they could have done*. They will interpret the conflict and their own bad behavior to conform to their values, a psychological process known as cognitive dissonance. **No matter what their politics or principles, religion or beliefs, *they will act against you* if they believe "your" problem might in any way become their own.**

If you are being mobbed in a context outside the workplace, such as among your church group, a club, a community or even a family, these same concepts apply. Every group, however loosely organized, has its formal and informal leaders and influencers, and by identifying those in your group you will better understand how and why they will respond as they do. By understanding how group aggression works and how leadership influences whether this aggression intensifies or gets put out at the first whiff of smoke, you can better protect yourself.

In the organizational culture of the workplace, however, at least if it is mid-sized or larger, there are two other important offices that shape the outcome of a mobbing. These are Human Resources (HR), and Affirmative Action or Diversity departments.

Most people who have been bullied or mobbed have a good understanding of the role HR plays in fueling aggression, but that understanding often comes too late—they have discovered the hard way that HR is not there to be a friend. As I've stated previously, HR works for management, not for employees. But in any conflict with management that comes with mobbing, HR is usually brought in to play an enforcing role—typically in the guise of "helping."

Make no mistake, no matter how kind and caring the personnel in HR may be, and many indeed are kind and caring, they are in a tenuous position. They have been charged with enforcing management's orders, and should they support a mobbing target who is a target of management-backed mobbing, they are expected to document the claims against the employee—to provide a paper trail legitimating the action which is sure to follow—a dismissal for cause. They are there to thwart any potential lawsuits by demonstrating that they did provide a service to the employee, they did "do something" about the employee's complaint, and they did act fairly.

They are not there to give serious consideration to "your problem," to tell management to knock it off and stop attacking you, or to change anybody's mind about you. Indeed, in a case of mobbing, if they did so they know they could be the next target.

Avoid HR at all costs and if you are compelled to cooperate with their office, do so knowing that anything you say can and will be used against you. Treat them with respect, keep your emotions in check, do not appear angry no matter how enraged you are, but **minimize your encounter with this office**. Do not ask them for anything—unless you have filed a complaint or grievance that requires you do so. (I'll get to how to do that in Chapter Five.)

But perhaps more confusing and complex in organizational hierarchies is the office of Affirmative Action. Mobbing commonly includes this office for two reasons: the mobbing target is "different," such as a member of a protected class (by race, gender, age, disability or sexuality), and much of the aggression against them is linked to their membership in this class, which is to say, it's unlawful discrimination.

The other reason is that mobbing often entails accusations against an employee that he or she has discriminated against someone in a protected class (such as charges of racism, sexism, or sexual harassment), and the office is conducting an investigation against the employee. Sometimes there is merit to the charges—sometimes the employee has acted in a blatantly discriminatory and unlawful manner. Often there is either nothing, or a little bit of something to it, a "politically incorrect" comment, a little too much flattery toward the opposite sex, what have you. In those cases, which most often can be dealt with effectively and efficiently by a simple but direct conversation, **the role of the Affirmative Action office can become deadly**.

One of the best depictions of how a "politically incorrect" comment destroyed someone's career through the actions of administrative investigations is in the novel, *The Human Stain* by Philip Roth (which has also been made into a movie starring Anthony Hopkins). In my view, this novel is all that ever needs to be written in fiction on what mobbing is and does;

it is a superb illustration of how maddening and illogical mobbing is, and how devastating its results.

Another, lesser known, non-fiction account of mobbing is *The First Stone* by Helen Garner, which details the charges against a professor for allegedly fondling two female students. In this account, Garner shows how the office of Affirmative Action contributed to the spreading of rumors and distortion of the facts as it pursued a sexual harassment investigation against the professor.

What both of these books bring to light is the way in which a rumor can become a grievous indictment against someone and used to destroy a career and a human. Yet not only can it destroy the person who is accused, it can also destroy the accuser. That is because, like HR, these investigative offices are not independent of management. They are there for management—to justify terminations, to quash potential lawsuits, and to provide a veneer of doing something about discrimination and sexual harassment in the workplace. They answer to management, not to employees, and not to outside agencies.

More importantly, they are staffed by people who rarely have training in investigative methods. They usually do not know how to ask follow up questions, to accurately assess nonverbal language, or to phrase questions in a manner that will illicit an accurate and honest answer. More often than not they ask leading questions in an accusatory or overly sympathetic tone, making clear their bias. They do not ask follow up questions to vague statements unless doing so would support their foregone conclusion. They record their notes in a manner which uses the information they obtain selectively, to support the conclusion management wants from them, or which they assume management wants from them.

They lie to the people they are speaking to with false assurances of objectivity, fairness, and empathy, knowing full well the decision of who is at fault has already been made. In short, Affirmative Action offices rarely hire people who are qualified and prepared to conduct objective and competent investigations. They hire yes-men who have ideological commitments to diversity, but that doesn't mean they can recognize discrimination if it hits them in the face, much less non-discriminatory actions or god-forbid some nuance.

They are deemed qualified to conduct internal investigations because they have degrees in education, social work, business, organizational psychology, or human resources. They will have had cursory training in investigation and interviewing techniques, but it will rarely be of the quality that would effectively and objectively distinguish the truth from the lies, the rumors from the facts, much less the fuzzy middle. In short, most investigators with Affirmative Action offices couldn't find a Gideon's Bible in a Motel Six—unless management told them to find it.

Here's how they work: they listen compassionately to your concerns, which they may or may not be secretly recording. They assure you that they will look into the matter, and they ask you for a list of your witnesses. Do not expect them to contact your witnesses—unless you have made a complaint against someone management already wants to be rid of. If that is the case, they will be sure to do so.

When you follow up, urging them to contact your witnesses before they are intimidated by management or their memories fade or they depart the workplace, you will be told that they will make the decisions about who to contact and when.

If any of the witnesses you point to do not work for your employer, or are former staff members, they will not be contacted. They will focus only on who currently works for the employer, so any past history of harassment with other women, or someone's past history of making false accusations, will not be of interest to them.

They will repeatedly tell you that they are fact finders and fair. If they work as a team, they may tell you they have a "Chinese Wall" separating what one investigator finds from another. This is hog wash. Do not believe it.

They will rapidly, if not from the first meeting with you, decide what the truth is, and their "investigations" will be focused on gathering evidence to support that version of the truth. Any evidence you provide that counters that argument will either be dismissed, or twisted to support the truth they've already decided upon.

They will begin by soliciting emails: yours and everybody else's that were sent by you, from you or mentioned you. And if they don't, you can bet they are doing so for the person you reported. Either way, it is putting your coworkers on edge because no one wants to turn over their emails. You will not be popular for having made them do so.

They will ostensibly operate in secret. You will be assured this is for your own protection. But what that means is they will be asking questions of management and your coworkers about you, dropping hints that it is something very serious, but not saying exactly what it is. This secrecy will lead to all sorts of rumors and speculation and fear, and quickly ignite the mobbing. If it hasn't started by the time you walk into an Affirmative Action office, it will start soon after.

And it's not because they're bad people. Almost everyone who goes to work in an Affirmative Action office is motivated by a desire to see a better, healthier more humane working environment for everyone.

But the role that has been created for them has been a very limiting one, and it has forced them to operate in a very weird manner. If you are being mobbed, they're going to not only be seeing you at your worst, but they'll be hearing lots of people say really bad things about you. It will shape their perceptions.

But what if they're on your side? In many cases, if you walk into an Affirmative Action office with a concern, you will find they will support you and take swift action against the offender. If this happens, you will be happy and relieved. But here's the thing.

If that happens, it is likely because management has either already wanted to get rid of the person and you've provided them fuel for going after him or her. Or because they are staffed by people who presume all complaints of discrimination or harassment are legitimate, and they rubber stamp every complaint as valid.

In either case, watch what happens to the person you reported. Watch as he or she is mobbed out the door or into a powerless position of submission. Is that really the best way to deal with a workplace conflict? Is that really the best way to show a person how hurtful or misguided their actions may have been? Think about it, because you just might be playing a role in someone's mobbing yourself.

Now if you think that Affirmative Action offices are all staffed by rabid feminists who will always back women, or that they see discrimination everywhere they look, stop right here. It is true that some are staffed by extremists, but that is rare. And if you already have your mind made up that all the women will unite against you or all the people of color will point their fingers at you accusing you of discrimination, and you find yourself hammering out comments on blog posts about how hateful these feminists/minorities/liberals/conservatives/men/white people are, you have already lost. Your anger is blinding you to potential allies, and making you vulnerable to potential enemies who will gun you down in a heartbeat even though they share your views. Here's what you need to know.

Women are no more united than men. Same goes for minorities. Each person will make their decisions based on their self-interest, not on their ideologies or social status. If you are certain no women will support you if you've been accused of sexual harassment, you are making a huge mistake. Many women, even feminists, will support you—either because they are rational and know a phony accusation or overreaction when they see it, or because they are happy to go after whoever it is who has made a charge against you. So don't start screaming about "feminists" or "sexist men." You'll alienate potential allies.

Moreover, if you think that by filing a sexual harassment or racial discrimination claim, that other women or people of color will support you, think again. They will be the first people your employer will court and shower with affection and perks. You cannot count on them. If your complaint has any merit, management is likely rewarding your potential allies with perks, raises and promotions to defeat your claims, and you probably won't even know it until it is too late. **Do not assume that people's social status as a member of any one gender, race, sexuality, age or what have you, will shape how they respond to you.**

So should you just avoid Affirmative Action offices altogether? If you possibly can, yes, absolutely. But you may not be able to. If you bring a complaint about protected acts to a supervisor, they may have to report it to the Affirmative Action office whether you like it or not. In most cases, they actually have some wiggle room and can deal with the matter with a conversation first, before having to take further action. But even if that's the case, chances are they *think* they have to report it. And whether or not they think they need to, they likely will. That is because by reporting it, they get it off their hands—they are no longer responsible for the conflict and do not have to do anything about it.

In other words, a relatively minor concern that you might want to handle with nothing more than a few words of sage advice or discussion, can rapidly turn into a major formal investigation aimed at destroying someone—maybe even you.

There is another reason that you may have to deal with the Affirmative Action office whether you want to or not. If you find yourself filing a complaint with the EEOC and/or involved in litigation against your employer, you must show that you have exhausted all internal remedies—which means HR and the Affirmative Action office.

In Chapter Five, I'll tell you more about how to do this, but for now, what you need to know is that the organizational culture in which you work is not the wonderful well-meaning institution you read about on your employer's website or Mission Statement. It has specific networks through which information and resources are exchanged, alliances forged, and opportunities created. And it is staffed by humans who have conflicting interests in promoting their own careers, doing "the right thing," and responding to the social cues they observe.

Think back to the ways that animals behave under stress or when observing their leader's behavior toward a vulnerable member of the group. When you come to others in the organizational culture for help, you're the screaming monkey. Stop screaming and start thinking. You need to be safe and sane.

In conclusion, by examining the organizational culture as a network of shifting alliances and interests, you are better able to protect yourself. Do not make the mistake of assuming your organization is "good" or "bad," or you may step on some landmines. This is another reason that the "bully" paradigm is flawed.

Just as it would have been absurd for Zimbardo to get rid of the bad guards in his Stanford prison experiment in hopes the aggressive behavior would be stopped, getting rid of the bullies in an institutional setting that has ignited and encouraged mobbing is an impossible task, given the number of aggressive participants. By shifting from a focus on bad apple bullies, to a focus on the institutional context that ignites group bullying or mobbing in the workplace, more effective workplace policies and practices become possible.

But to get there, we must dare to step beyond the boundaries of the individual bully paradigm, to consider how *group* psychology contributes to workplace aggression and turns good people bad. To do so, we might do well to mindfully step onto the path of workplace compassion. Instead of ridding the workplace of bullies, we might reflect on how we can contribute to a kinder, gentler way of working together. It begins not with how we treat those inside the golden circle, but how we treat those who've been cast from it.

So let's take a look at how that happens. Let's consider how the group responds when someone points the finger at a bully, or has the finger pointed at them, and who ends up cast out.

CHAPTER 3

How Mobbing Starts

So just how does this mobbing get started, and what does it entail? It starts like this: you do something to piss someone off. It's that plain and simple, really. What's not so simple is recognizing it when it happens. It can be something as trivial as voting the wrong way on what you think is a minor issue, or filing an objection to a harsh review that you think is just a formality to clarify the record. It might just be disagreeing with a superior about something they feel strongly about. You might not even realize you ticked someone off, at least not in any meaningful way.

Or it could be something big. You may have reported some misconduct; brought your supervisor's attention to an unethical practice going on; filed a complaint of discrimination; or been accused by someone else of some type of wrongdoing. Whatever it is that you have done, you will probably have no idea the ramifications until the mobbing is well underway.

"The incident—*the incident!*—provided them with an 'organizing issue' of the sort that was needed at a racially retarded place like Athena. Why did I quit? By the time I quit, it was essentially over." (Philip Roth 2000:17, emphasis in the original).

In *The Human Stain*, a novel by Philip Roth with a premise based on a true story, protagonist Coleman Silk describes the sudden downfall of his career of three decades after allegations of racism are filed against him. The incident? He had referred to two chronically absent students as "spooks," not knowing that they were Black. As the machinery of his professional destruction ensues and one by one his friends and colleagues turn against him, Silk discovers just how cruel and destructive mobbing can be, until his once-successful and much-loved career has been destroyed.

Yet prior to the accusation, there was nothing known about him that was considered troublesome or different—despite harboring a secret that led him to conceal any marker of difference. Instead, he did his best to assimilate and fit in. But once "the incident" led Coleman Silk to be singled out for persecution, his increasing isolation became viewed as evidence of his difference.

In many mobbing cases, however, there is a period before "the incident," in which the target is marked early on as somehow different. This difference might be visible, such as race or gender. It might be a worker who becomes perceived as weakened—the worker who is ill, the older worker who is perceived as no longer relevant, the uneducated and grossly underpaid clerical or staff member who isn't as hip and cool as the other workers, or the overweight worker who is perceived as lacking discipline and beauty. Or the difference might be a personal characteristic, such as a political ideology, religion, style of communicating, or a set of beliefs—something that differs in a noticeable way from the majority of the group.

If the difference that is perceived is viewed as a weakness, shunning will be the most damaging, but overt acts of aggression may be limited. If difference is perceived as something other than a weakness, however, the difference itself might not initially be a great concern, but it is something that raises the alarm among the group that *this is someone to be watched*.

Let's assume you're that someone. Over time, if you fit in, the difference ceases to matter; like Coleman Silk, you belong. But if you should ever do something to rub someone the wrong way—someone who is in a position of leadership or influence—this difference becomes significant. It confirms the fear that had already been subtly (or not so subtly) felt among the group. No one is likely to come out and say anything derogatory about you based on that difference, but what happens is a growing sense that *you're not one of us* starts to take hold.

Thus, anything you do or say that brings attention to the fact that you are not one of them, is liable to be noted. Should you do or say something that leads to someone in a position of authority wanting you gone, or provokes the machinery of human resources or any form of investigation, you had best be on guard for a mobbing.

Here's how it works. Let's say someone is bullying you, maybe even bullying several people, and they are in a managerial position, or have influence over someone who is in management. You often bitch about this person to your colleagues, sharing stories of their latest bad behavior, and everyone agrees, this jerk is just plain mean. Then one day, they go too far. They do something so abusive that you can no longer keep your mouth shut. You file a complaint, certain that your friends and colleagues will stand behind you, since they've endured the same crap.

Or let's say, someone files a complaint against *you*. They accuse *you* of being the bully, and you're astounded—because you've never been abusive to anyone. Sure, you've lost your temper every now and then, but you are hardly a bully. Or someone said you said something racist or sexist or homophobic, and you're shocked. Or someone accused you of sexual harassment, and you have no idea how they could call your behavior harassing. Or someone said you did something dishonest, unethical or against the law. Whatever it was, the accusation has shocked you, but you are confident that your work record will speak for itself. No one in their right mind would believe you would ever intentionally do such a thing, and you are certain that whatever crap management puts you through as a result, your friends and colleagues will stand behind you, since they know you're a decent person.

Or let's say the jerk of a boss just denied your promotion and you've filed a grievance. Or fired you without good reason and you're going to fight for reinstatement. Or hired his mistress, and you're going to object because he's paying her triple your salary. Whatever it is, you've found yourself reluctantly having to file a complaint against management, but you aren't worried because the law is on your side. The boss violated procedure or even your contract, and you know she screwed up and you can prove it. He demonstrated just how abusive, punitive and bullying he can be. She deliberately targeted you in violation of the law or at the very least the rules laid out in the employee handbook, because you're a minority, the only white guy, a woman, a man, a conservative, a liberal, gay, not gay, outspoken, or shy. Whatever the reason, it was wrong, it was unfounded, and you know you'll get it overturned because your friends and colleagues will stand behind you since this kind of crap could happen to them if it's not exposed.

Whatever the details, you have been thrust into the machinery of the organization, and you're angry and quite possibly shocked, but you are confident of one thing—your friends and colleagues will stand behind you (well, except for a few you know will gun you down first chance they get, but your friends, at least, will be on your side, that much you can count on).

But here's what's going on behind the scenes. Once you come to someone in management with a complaint, or a complaint has been made against you, the person receiving the complaint will do one of two things. They will handle the matter swiftly and fairly, not make a big deal of it, settle it and move on. That probably won't happen if it is referred, by you or by them, to an affirmative action office. But if it's just an internal matter and your manager is a decent person, chances are, it will be quickly resolved.

What *might* happen, if you are in that "different" category and/or have annoyed them (intentionally or not) in the past, is they will resolve the matter, but make a note of it in a file, which you may never know of. They may even mention something to someone above them, and/or someone alongside them but who is above you in the organizational hierarchy. If they do so, it will be mentioned almost casually, but presented in a manner to alert that person that you are a potential troublemaker, but that *this time*, they've taken care of it. The message is clear: let's keep our eye on this troublemaker. In this scenario, you are likely to think the matter was resolved and all is well. You are unlikely to know that you've had your first (or second) strike, and the third will get you out.

If the matter is not swiftly and fairly resolved informally, and you or someone else is demanding action be taken to resolve it, this is what will happen. The person you report your problem to will go to the person above him or her—in other words, they will ask their supervisor what to do. But before they do so, *they will have already decided what they want to do.* They will decide *you* are a troublemaker and need to go, or they will decide the other person involved—the person who reported you, or the person you reported—is a troublemaker and needs to go.

Now *here's where you have to pay attention*—the decision of who has to go will not be based on logic. It will probably not be based on the nature of the accusation, on the actual damage that was sustained, on fairness or on facts. **The decision of who will go will be based on who is the least costly politically to dispense with, or who they most dislike.**

We tend to think that fairness and logic prevail in these sorts of situations, so if you come to your boss with a problem, they're going to want to take care of it, especially if the problem is damaging the organization in a small or bigger way. But that's not how it always happens. As I've suggested, if they are a confident and humane manager, they will simply resolve the problem quickly and effectively. But if they're a Worried Killer, a Jackal, or a Jack Ass—or just one of those managers who squirms at confrontation—something else will happen.

What happens is they will immediately take sides. They will decide who they like working with more—you or the other person. And if there is no identifiable "other person" in the dispute, they will decide whether or not they want to keep working with you. **It is not likely to make much difference how valuable you are.** We all overestimate out value to the workplace, and underestimate how easily we're replaced.

Another thing your boss is going to do is he or she will very likely calculate how bad exposing the problem will make them look, and which remedy will win them favor with the folks above them. So **when they go to their boss, they will present the problem in a manner which casts the troublemaker as whoever they want to go**—not on who is actually causing the trouble. They will then ask what to do about the troublemaker, and they will be told to get rid of the troublemaker. They will be told to document the incident, alert the proper internal agencies, and instruct any relevant assistants of what is going on and to be discreet.

What this means is they will be following orders from their boss—just doing as they've been told. **They are no longer responsible for what happens next**; they're just responsible for making sure it happens and that's what they will do. And it means something else—it means word will extend upward in management of who has to go, and it will extend horizontally among management. In other words, every level of warlord will alert his or her guards that a troublemaker is on the loose and has to be restrained.

All that follows will then be predetermined by various employees, managers and investigators *following orders from their boss*. The orders won't be to hear the parties out, consider the facts, or make any effort to resolve the matter constructively. The orders will be to use their power to quash the troublemaker. And whoever the target for elimination is—which very likely is you—they will be assured that proper procedures will be followed and all will be fair and above-board.

As for you, after presenting your complaint or concern, you will be told everything is fine; they're taking care of it, don't worry. When that happens, you will likely assume that whatever stress you are under, who the troublemaker is in the dispute is clear—whoever you reported, or whoever reported you. If you made the report, chances are you won't assume it's you. If someone else made the report against you, you will worry about what's coming down and what's going to happen to your reputation, but you will likely assume they'll be exposed as the troublemaker and all will be well in the end.

It is very important at this stage—and at all stages—that you not presume that just because your employer and/or coworkers are strongly opposed to bullying, racism, sexism, homophobia or whatever that they will act in accordance with their principles. This is such an important point that it can't be repeated enough—**never assume that it is safe to report sexual harassment to a woman, or racism to a person of color, or bullying behavior to someone who has no tolerance for bullies, just because of their gender, race or stated values. The actions which follow will not be based on ethics, principles or on facts, but on the fictions that follow as the conflict turns into gossip and gossip turns into "facts."**

As the days follow any formal report, unless you've been a paragon of discretion, gossip is likely to circulate. You are likely to want to tell your side of the story, especially if others are involved and telling their sides of the story. And when you tell your side at this point, people will listen sympathetically, and some might even be outraged, and even share their own stories.

But **talking about it will do four things to damage you**: it will give you the false confidence that others are on your side; it will tempt you to reveal information you would be better off not disclosing; it will give rise to future claims against you as what you said is distorted into something entirely different; and it will get you madder than hell.

It will get you madder than hell because *the more you tell your story, the more you will relive it.* And when we relive an experience, we relive all the emotions we felt when it originally happened. The more we *think* about it and the more we *talk* about it, the more powerful it becomes. No one ever says, "The more I thought about it, the less important it became." The more we think about something, the bigger it becomes. So it's at this stage—when management is first alerted there's a problem and people start talking about it—that the "problem" begins to take on a life of its own—in the organization, and in your mind.

We'll get to how to safeguard your mind later on, but first, let's stay focused on the organization. Something else will also be going down in the organization while you do all your gossiping and thinking about this problem, so you'd better be on your toes.

Here's what's going to happen. People will be called into the boss's office or the boss will drop in on them. These meetings are likely to be discreet and in most cases, will ostensibly be for some other reason. (If your mobbing isn't work-related, then whoever is in a position of influence will engage in a similar strategy, primarily through gossip channels.) Here's how those discreet meetings will go.

"Hey, Larry, do you have a minute? I just took a look at your report and it looks great."

"Sure!" Larry says, excited to hear the boss tell him how brilliant he is. He'll step into the office, and be told to close the door, or the boss will step into Larry's office, and casually close the door.

The conversation will then proceed about Larry's report, wrapping up with some informal chit chat. And that's when Larry will be asked about the troublemaker—which is to say, you or the one you think is the troublemaker—which is the office bully/lothario/racist/whatever.

"Oh, one more thing," the boss will say as he or she is wrapping up the conversation, "I know you've probably heard some things lately about so-and-so's problem . . ." In framing it this way, Larry will already be primed by the alpha on *who* has—and thus is—the problem.

Larry will be told there is indeed something going on, but the boss—who raised the issue—can't talk about it. It will be implied that there is more to it than Larry has heard. This possibility is always suggested because it is critical to shaping Larry's views. Whether Larry likes you or not, he may well have an opinion that in management's eyes could need changing, so by suggesting there is "new information" of unknown content, Larry has wiggle room to change his views. But for the time being, all that needs to be done is for the boss to plant the seed, not change his views or get him to commit to any position—except for one, very minor one—and that is that whatever the conflict is, it's unfairly affected Larry.

The boss will express "concern," for Larry having to be exposed to it—by way of being the troublemaker's friend, coworker, or target. Larry will agree that it has been difficult. And that's all the boss needed to hear. If

Larry is not a friend, this is where Larry will readily vent, and assure the boss he agrees this person needs to go. If that's the case, not much more needs to be said. The boss has him in his hands. Larry will bring him a steady stream of gossip, testify against the troublemaker, and cooperate with his elimination.

But if Larry is a friend, all he did was agree that it's been difficult, which it has. Larry's had to hear his friend babble and rant for ages and he's so tired of it. Larry's worried that if management comes after his friend, he might be in the line of fire. Larry's worried he might have to testify or answer uncomfortable questions. So what's the big deal if he agreed that yes, it has been difficult.

It's a big deal psychologically, because it's what's called a "small betrayal"—one which will make bigger betrayals all the more easy—and one which is essential if Larry is a close friend.

If Larry is indeed a close friend or close coworker, he will also be told that the boss 1) knows of the friendship or alliance; 2) respects that friendship/alliance and would not do anything to jeopardize it; 3) wants Larry to know there are some other things that have happened that he doesn't know about (hints of more "new information" to come;) and 4) knows this person has been unhappy for some time and would really be so much happier somewhere else. This is where **the boss will sing the praises of the person he or she is planning to eliminate, and assure Larry that everything will be handled fairly**.

Larry will be relieved to hear the boss respects his friendship with someone in the line of fire, a bit curious to know what the other information is that hasn't been shared with him by his friend, and in agreement that his friend is really unhappy. As he's feeling all these things, he will be assured that he doesn't have to worry about any fallout affecting him, asked not to say anything because it's all under investigation, and by the way, that raise/promotion/office perk/day off/vacation/whatever it is that Larry has wanted, just might be on its way.

Larry will leave with a smile—happy that something good is coming his way, confident about the report the boss sought him out to discuss, and slightly ashamed he agreed that his friend or colleague was such a problem, but, after all, it has been a pain having to listen to these last few days or weeks or even months. Oh, well, that's someone else's problem. Larry's in good with the boss.

If the allegation you make or has been made against you has anything to do with race/gender/sexuality/religion or any other status that is protected by federal civil rights laws, members of that class will be among the first to be courted by management in this respect. **Expect that if there is an allegation of discrimination made, that regardless of past patterns of discrimination, members of that class will receive new resources, opportunities, raises and promotions**.

Now these conversations will take place with almost all the employees, with slight variation. If the boss is confident that Larry will share the view of who it is that needs to go, the conversation will be a little more frank—maybe a lot more. Depending on Larry's character and place in the organization, he may be more directly told that the troublemaker has to go. But for the most part, those conversations will have the following characteristics:

- They will be seemingly informal and often ostensibly about something else (giving plausible deniability that the meetings ever happened);
- They will take place behind closed doors with no other witnesses;
- They will include assurances that the employee they're speaking with is doing well and can expect nothing but support from management;
- They will be assured that the boss understands how difficult the other person's problem has become for them and for the entire workforce;
- They will be assured that the matter will be resolved and that something good is on the horizon.

So given that this is how the first stage of mobbing commences, if you report someone to management or someone reports something about you, how will you know if you're the target or if they are? It has nothing to do with what you reported or what the facts are. If you're brought in for a similar talk with the boss like the one I just discussed shortly after the incident has been raised, then chances are, you'll start seeing "the other person" look stressed and increasingly isolated, while things start looking up for you. You will have come away from that talk with the boss feeling good and looking forward to someone else being gone. Intentionally, knowingly or not, you'll become a part of a mob to eliminate someone else.

But if the boss doesn't drop by to chat with you in an openly friendly manner or invite you into his or her office with a broad smile in the wake of making the report and begins to avoid you—then be forewarned—*you are about to be mobbed.*

What exactly does that mean? As mobbing commences, your coworkers will initially seek you out for information. They will feign support and interest in your views. They may well call you at home or even drop by, appearing empathetic as they pepper you with questions.

It won't be long, however, before they distance themselves from you, while at the same time their gossip will turn to damaging rumors and speculation against you, which in turn will lead to false reports being made to management of all sorts of horrible or crazy or outlandish or suspicious or dangerous or dishonest or stupid things you have allegedly done. Eventually, as they continue to avoid you, your coworkers may refuse to cooperate or work with you, they will keep important information from you and deprive you of other resources necessary to do your job. In short order you will be subjected to a series of secretive investigations, damaging evaluations, allegations of misconduct, and workplace surveillance as your emails are monitored, your offices and phones searched, and your work scrutinized for errors. In almost all cases you will either be moved to a remote office, demoted to a less responsible position—usually in another location—encouraged to take time off, or just not included in any group meeting or event. Rendering you invisible will be essential to maintaining the aggression against you—the less they actually have to interact with you, the easier it will be to talk about you.

But here's the thing. **You are not likely to recognize the mobbing initially, because most of what will go down at first will take place behind closed doors.** If there is any formal investigation, you will be assured they will do a full investigation, you have nothing to worry about as long as you're telling the truth, and that you are not to discuss the matter with anyone. The first phase will be almost a relief in many cases—because you will be so repeatedly assured that everything will be resolved and you needn't worry.

One reason you are unlikely to recognize the mobbing until it's gained momentum is because up until the shunning begins, your friends will be eager to hear your side of the story. And if there's any sort of investigation, which there almost always is, even though you've been told not to talk about it, you'll want to prepare a few people in case they are contacted and asked about what they know. You'll try not to say much, but you'll still be stressed, and you'll probably talk more than you should, but still, you'll be assured by the responses of your friends that all is well. But little by little, you'll note some changes.

- Your boss will only talk to you when necessary;
- No one will ask you for any favors, to work with them on any projects, or put you on any committees—and should you volunteer, you'll be cheerfully thanked but passed up;
- There won't be any social events—you may not notice this at first, but if there are usually after-hours social events, you'll start to realize there haven't been many in a while. Eventually, they'll resume, but you won't be invited (don't bother to ask about them, you'll be told no one else was invited either, it was just a small affair, or that you were sent an invitation and must have lost it);
- Other people you work with, particularly your friends or close colleagues, will be put on committees, given important assignments,

or receive other perks—you won't hear about the raises or promotions at first, but over time, you will;

- People who once spent time with you no longer will, and pretty soon, you'll notice they close the door when you approach, turn away, or gossip in clusters with glances over to you;
- Any resources you request will be denied, your work may be outright sabotaged, you may be moved to a remote location, you may come to work to discover your computer was turned on, your office door unlocked;
- Others will be credited with your work achievements;
- You will be subjected to a series of accusations and investigations (more on those later);
- You will think you are losing your mind, you will become a complete mess, your work will suffer, you will think incessantly of the wrong that was done you and the cruelty and unfairness of what is happening, and you will be desperate for it to stop.

As the incident that first led you to step into the organizational sinkhole turns into a mobbing, you will turn to your friends and closest colleagues for support—both personally and strategically—and you will convince yourself that they are on your side far longer than they will actually be on your side. Because just like Larry, they've all turned against you, and while you might recognize the signs early on from the ones who were never very close, the ones closest to you will still be there. They may not be there as often as you like, they may not call you as often or invite you to join them for lunch or activities outside of work, but when you call them, they'll listen to you babble. They'll assure you that you are being screwed and they care. And they'll encourage you to quit and move on, and that will piss you off, because you should not be the one who has to leave. But here's what you need to know:

Management will have already recruited your closest friends and colleagues at an early stage for several reasons.

By persuading your friends to turn away from you, you will lose critical social support. You will become isolated which increases your stress and undermines your work performance and emotional stability, making it easier to justify your termination.

Your friends have intimate information about you which can be used against you. They may know intimate details about you and your life, they may know where any skeletons are buried, they may know your weak spots, they may know any legal or administrative strategy you are planning to take, and they likely know what stupid things you've said about management, the organization, other workers, or anything else that can be used against you.

Other observers will be more likely to side against you and believe management's version of events once your own friends turn against you—after all, if even your own friends are fed up, then you must have it coming.

Friends are the most emotionally exhausted by you because they've been hearing you babble and bitch for ages, they're scared of being the next target, and they just want it to be over—in most cases, your friends are easier to persuade to join management than most impartial observers, but most people do not understand this fact, which makes courting your friends all the more effective.

Your friends will influence the gossip in important respects by sharing their "concern" about you, and encouraging others to do the same. They will subtly begin to tip the gossip from any problems you are having with management or someone else, to seeing the problem as arising from you. They will not be obvious about it—they will present it as if whatever the merits of your position, they are "concerned" that you are not thinking clearly—which others will eagerly agree with because they, too, have had closed door conversations with management. (And because as the mobbing progresses, you won't be thinking clearly.) In this way, your "friends" not only shape the gossip to turn against you, but in their retelling of it they begin to revise the story to fit management's version of events—and thereby justify their own growing alliance with management.

Friends will keep their mouth shut about what management is up to longer than others—they will not let you know they're confiding in management, they will continue to pretend they are friends because they will be ashamed and fearful of the truth being revealed, and they will discover that by continuing to pretend to be your friend they will continue to be emotionally exhausted by you (thereby justifying their betrayal), *and they will continue to receive valuable information that can be passed on to management*—and thereby improve their own status in the organization. Ironically, they will also be praised for being such a "good friend"—because they will continue to claim to care and be concerned, but they are also worn out. In this way, they foster an image that they are a victim of your abuse, while systematically betraying you at a time when you are most in need of support and genuine friendship (but you're not entirely off the hook here, in Chapter Seven I discuss how your behaviors are indeed wearing others out and what you need to do to change that).

Finally, and most importantly, once it is impossible for your friend to hide their betrayal any longer—usually after management has taken action on information the friend has provided—they will prove to be *extremely* aggressive. There are two reasons for their heightened aggression.

The first is that they will want to quash any uncomfortable feelings of shame, so through the psychological process of cognitive dissonance, it will be essential that they convince not just others, but themselves, that what they did was two things—one, necessary, and two, the *only* thing they could have done. To do so, they will accuse you of *always* having been a problem, and like an ugly divorce, they will completely revise your identity and the history of your friendship.

They are likely to claim they've always found you mentally unstable, and begin to cast your friendship as anything but mutual—*they* were being friendly to *you* and tried very hard to befriend you despite your constant problems. Another spin on this one is that you *were* friends, but there was something about you that you kept hidden—they didn't know about your racist side, they were unaware of how you treated women, they didn't know you were mentally ill. None of these descriptions of you need to be accurate. They just need to be alleged. The idea will be to acknowledge they were your friend, but only because they didn't know you well enough, and now that they do, they've had to end it.

The second thing your friends will do is take any and all action to discredit you so badly that anything you say or do in retaliation—such as disclose your former friend's own secrets or bad behaviors—will be ignored because no one will take them seriously.

In short, **the people you most need and trust to back you up will not only be the most likely to do you harm, but the harm they cause will be the most damaging you will suffer**. For this reason, it is imperative you keep your distance from them when mobbing is on the horizon. At the earliest sign of trouble, step back from your friendships. I tell you how to do so, and how to preserve those friendships, in Chapter Seven.

But for now, just know this: **thinking about people in terms of good or bad, or seeing them as bullies, does you absolutely no good in the midst of a mobbing**. That's because in mobbing even the good go bad— and the closer they are, the badder they'll go. So drop that bully thinking right here and now because yes, some people are bullies, but if you focus on them and their behavior, you're going to miss the real damage that's coming your way—from the ones who've never bullied but have become convinced that *you're* poisoning the workplace. And why are they so certain that you're the one causing all the problems? Because everybody says so.

CHAPTER 4

Gossip, Rumors and Accusations

"Want to ruin a person?" asks Phil Porter in his book, *Eat or Be Eaten: Jungle Warfare for the Master Corporate Politician*, "Start rumors – any sort of rumor. People will want to believe it. If enough do, it becomes true, even if it is totally untrue. You can't escape the opinions of the masses, regardless of how erroneous they are."

"Sometimes you'll need to leak information or spread ideas that damage somebody else's reputation," writes managerial consultant Joep Schrijvers in his best-selling book, *The Way of the Rat: A Survival Guide to Office Politics*, "either way, you must stay in the background and let rumors, whispers, and back-room gossip do their work. Leaks call for timing, character assassination needs to be kept up constantly."

Mobbing is the elephant in the room when someone is targeted for elimination, the thing few speak about, but most have witnessed in one form or another—the collective glee that a group of people feel when they have been given permission to bad mouth, damage and hurt another person.

Once mobbing is underway, the ones in management who instigated it needn't do anything more. They know that between gossip and the internal investigations, whatever story they want to spin will stick. They've done their damage; now it's time for the machinery of the organization—and the gossip mill—to get to work. But how it starts is subtle.

Based on his Stanford Prison Experiments, psychologist Philip Zimbardo has noted that there is a slippery slope of evil that begins with mindlessly taking the first step toward aggression through a seemingly minor action. Similarly, when mobbing begins workers are not initially encouraged to be cruel to the targeted worker. Far from it; they are told that the worker will be better off if they just move on, that the job is a bad fit, and that any problems are really the worker's own doing.

As we've seen with our make-believe coworker, Larry, the first step onto the slippery slope of mobbing behavior often begins with something as simple as agreeing with management that the targeted worker must go—even if the decision to terminate the worker is clearly arbitrary or punitive or in some cases illegal, such as retaliation for reporting sexual harassment, discrimination or unlawful behavior. *It's for their own good*, coworkers are assured—even if losing their job will present a serious hardship and future work will be difficult to obtain for the mobbing target. *Everything always turns out for the best; they'll find something better . . .*

How are people persuaded to take that first step onto the slippery slope and agree their coworker must go? With new information. By dropping the suggestion that "there's more to it" than they've been told, management sows doubt. By telling the coworker that the targeted employee had criticized them sometime in the past or stabbed them in the back—whether true or not. Anything can be made up to divide and conquer the group. And by letting the gossip mill do its thing, that mythical "new information" becomes real—people *will* start reporting things, even things that never happened. And as anyone who gossips know, the more a rumor or piece of gossip is passed on, the more it's embellished until the final story is so outlandish that not even Stephen King could fathom such an ending.

But they won't do that to me, you might think; they all know I'm right. I have an impeccable record. I'm very popular. My friends and coworkers have integrity and they know that I do, too. All they need to hear is my side of the story.

That's where you're wrong. By the time the gossip starts flowing, your coworkers will no longer think you're right. They'll think you're a pain in the ass who should have kept your mouth shut. By the time mobbing is underway, your record is no longer impeccable. Everyone knows you never deserved any accolades. You got so many good reviews and raises and promotions because you're a minority/a woman/a white man. Because they bent over backwards to give you what you wanted. Because you cheated or bullied or scammed or slept your way to the top. Or because you're too ambitious and will do anything to get to the top. One by one your achievements will be replaced by every mistake you ever made and a whole lot you never made as people recount your history with them.

Popular? Not anymore. Nobody's ever really liked you, they'll say. You're superficially charming. You're a sociopath who manipulates people into doing your bidding. People were nice to you because they were afraid of you. So what if people liked and admired you. Nobody's friends with you now (not even your own friends—they've told us what you're *really* like and now we feel sorry for *them*). Integrity? You're lying about this whole thing—everyone knows that manager you bitched so much about was never a bully—she was only reacting to *you*. And if we ever agreed with you about her, it's only because you manipulated us into thinking that way. Your side of the story? We've heard it till we're sick to death; maybe we bought it for awhile, but now we know better.

In other words, no matter who you are or what your work record or reputation is, once you are a target of mobbing, you can and will be taken down. Here's how.

Gossip and Rumors

We tend to use the terms gossip and rumors interchangeably, but they're actually two different things. Rumors are specific pieces of information that may well be truthful, and are often at least partially true. Rumors circulate in environments where information is controlled; they are unsubstantiated pieces of information that arise in contexts of ambiguity, secrecy or threats. For this reason, they are particularly fertile at two stages of mobbing—the early "pre-mobbing" stage when "the incident" is about to erupt, or has just erupted; and the crisis stage, when the mobbing has commenced, management has alerted the workforce that something is happening and that they are expected to cooperate with managerial objectives (in other words, help get the target out), and the target has been effectively shunned and excluded from social circles (an essential element to mobbing, because in order for a unified version of events to gain momentum, the person they are talking about must be absent).

Rumors are intended to transmit relevant information to workers which will help them make sense of the uncertainty swirling around the workplace. They answer such questions as: What happened? When did it happen? Who did it happen to? Why did it happen? Who is to blame? What will happen next?

Consequently, if you are having a conflict with someone at work, and considering reporting the conflict to your manager, or someone else is considering reporting you to management, rumors will begin to spread. At this stage, they are likely to be at least partially truthful, and if you are the one who is about to make the report, they are likely to be favorable to you.

On the other hand, if someone else is about to report you to management, or has just done so, they very well may be damaging rumors that will not support you. **The psychology of accusation leads us to distance ourselves from the one accused, so whoever is accused of a wrongdoing is at a disadvantage in this early stage of rumors**.

In contrast to rumors, gossip is comprised of evaluative statements about a person's character and private life. Whereas rumors are usually distinct pieces of information relevant to the group, gossip is purely judgmental, and will include generalized information about a person's character that has nothing to do with the group. The aim of gossip is to manage the status of the one gossiped about, to elevate or, more commonly, demote a person on the social status hierarchy. Gossip legitimates punishments, including shunning, by fostering a shared view that the person gossiped about is undeserving of respect, dignity, and humanity—and deserving of aggression (and once a target is deemed deserving of aggression, humans will always escalate their aggression).

Gossip serves another important social function—like rumors, it transmits information (however unrelated to the group it may be), but it also provides cohesion to the group, extends insider status to those who are privy to its contents, communicates group expectations and norms, and establishes, maintains or changes power structures within the group. For this reason, once "the incident" has passed, the initial rumors clarified, and the mobbing is well underway, gossip will fly as members become nervous of their own status in the organization and fearful of what might happen next. By uniting through gossip, tensions are eased and a shared version of events, judgment of the players, and justification for the aggression is fostered. Moreover, no one will consider their behavior as aggression, as bullying, as mobbing or as shunning. They will regard it as "deserved."

So what does this mean for you if you are being mobbed? It means that in the early stages, as rumors circulate they will be at least partially credible, and focused on something that matters to the workforce. Once the cat is out of the bag and whatever the incident was that sparked the mobbing has passed and the internal investigations have commenced, however, an atmosphere of secrecy will give rise to greater tension.

People will be told not to talk about the issue, while at the same time, they will be asked to turn over any emails or other communications sent to, received by, or mentioning you. Many will be told they may have to appear as witnesses or testify regarding what they know about the incident. **The rumors that arise during this stage will rapidly shift from the transmission of relevant information to critical judgment against whoever it is that management has targeted**. The rumors contained in the gossip will not be based on credible information at this point, but on speculation that will best fit leadership's aims. Importantly, **at this stage more and more people will move from the periphery of gossip circles to the center, as bystanders turn, one by one, into participants**.

If the target is you, the rumors which may have been initially supportive of you will rapidly shift to gossip about your character, integrity, mental status, and value not just as a worker, but as a human. In addition, **as gossip and rumors spread, they will become increasingly homogenized so that a single, shared interpretation of the characters and story line becomes agreed upon**. Anyone who questions the gossip or rumors, or who adds nuance, context, or challenging details, will be disliked—so people soon learn just how to present information about you and the conflict so that it is favorably received by the group. By doing so, they reinforce the accepted story line—that *you* have a problem and that you *are* the problem.

At the same time, you will be kept out of the loop. You won't know when your coworkers have had talks with management, though you will suspect they've probably been told something. You won't know about the raises and perks and benefits doled out, at least not right away. You'll notice some people have gotten some good things, but unless it's impossible to conceal, you won't know what goodies your coworkers have gotten. People will keep quiet about these things around you. But you're going to know that people have been told management's versions of events. So you'll want to give your side of the story.

You'll want to explain certain things, to clarify them. But doing so is a big mistake. **Anything you say can and will be used against you.** It doesn't matter whether what you say includes evidence to support you or counter the gossip. **Whatever you say at this stage will be exaggerated and distorted** to fit one of two explanatory models: 1) that you're crazy and/or dangerous and 2) that you're making even more accusations. Any detail you supply which clarifies something, which completely alters a rumor to support your position, *will be neglected in the retelling.* You could say that yes, you did come up behind someone and give them a bear hug as you shoved your fist hard in their gut, but they were choking on a chicken bone and you were giving the Heimlich maneuver and saved their life. The story that will be told, however, is that you ran up behind someone, grabbed them and punched them—and the person whose life you saved will forget all about the chicken bone and only remember the punch in the gut.

Similarly, any joke you tell will not be considered funny, even if they laugh when you tell it. Self-deprecating humor will be retold as if you have no self-confidence or are mentally unstable and sarcasm will be treated as if literal. A comment as casual as "This is one of those days when I should have just stayed in bed," will be turned into an admission that you planned to stay in bed and were complaining about having to come to work, that you are lazy, that you are so depressed you can't get out of bed. A sarcastic comment such as, "Where's Dexter when you need him?" referring to the popular serial killer TV character will be told as if you planned or threatened to kill someone.

In other words, **if you are mobbed a single storyline will be told and it will favor whoever has power, regardless of the facts, regardless of what you do or say, and regardless of your intentions. The story will support the conclusion that you must go, and that anything anyone does to you or says about you, is nobody's fault but your own**.

This is where cognitive dissonance kicks in again. As people gossip adversely against you, they won't want to notice anything about you that reminds them that you were their friend or respected colleague, that you are human and hurting and kind and undeserving of this treatment. That would be uncomfortable. What we do when we gossip is seek out evidence that reaffirms our view that the person we're gossiping about deserves it. And as we gossip, we tend to cloak our bad behavior in a slight admission of shame ("I shouldn't be saying this, but . . .") or acknowledgement of the subject's humanity ("Bless her heart . . ."), thereby giving us the green light to go ahead and gossip.

As the rumors slow and the gossip grows old, people will look to the past for new tidbits to add to the gossip. They will rethink past interactions with you, and no matter how enjoyable they may have been at the time, they will remember them in a new light. Just as someone divorcing relives their entire marriage and tells story after story from the past demonstrating what a bad person their future ex-spouse is, your coworkers will start retelling stories from the past that paint you in a negative light, removing context, nuance and any details that would portray you as sane and caring and trustworthy and competent. They are trying to find evidence to justify their own bad behavior in shamelessly putting you down. And finding that evidence, they'll heave a sigh of relief, and carry on talking about how awful you are until they no longer have you in their lives.

That's what's going to happen to you if leadership gives the green light to your elimination. Here's how it goes:

Let's say the target is a guy named Steve, who has been with the organization for several years, has been well-liked among most, but over the years has occasionally crossed paths with this or that person along the way, always amicably resolving any conflicts. His work record is excellent, and he has measurable achievements which have benefitted the organization.

A management position opens up and a few internal candidates are considered. Steve openly supports promoting Theresa to the position and many of his colleagues agree that she would be the best person for the job, particularly since few women have been promoted to management. Theresa herself is eager for the position, and appreciative of Steve for his support. Another candidate for the position, Ron, gets the position, however, and Steve grumbles among his coworkers that gender discrimination may have played a role in Theresa not getting the job, particularly because Ron's qualifications were not as strong as Theresa's.

But life goes on, and Steve does his best to get along with his new boss, Ron. But Ron, who previously didn't have any problems with Steve, resents the fact that Steve not only didn't back him, but suggested he was less qualified than Theresa and his promotion was discriminatory. He overlooks Steve for opportunities, dismisses his contributions in meetings, criticizes his reports, and gives him adverse performance reviews. Others also complain that Ron is not fair in his evaluations, treats them badly and that he is a lousy manager. Two of them quit, saying they can't take it anymore. The consensus soon emerges that Ron is a bully boss who was promoted because he was a male—and a suck up to the regional manager—and that productivity in the workplace is suffering and they are losing their top talent.

Steve's work suffers, he begins to hate his job, and every day seems to be another opportunity for Ron to criticize him. But he can't leave—he would lose his seniority and he's only ten years from retirement—it would also be hard for him to find a comparable job at his age, and he would probably have to relocate to do so—not easy with a wife who has her own career, and his kids in high school.

Finally, after a particularly brutal public bashing by Ron during a staff meeting, Steve files a grievance against him, alleging Ron's a bully. His co-workers encourage he do so, pointing out that it had been going on too long and something has to be done. Steve doesn't really want any formal issue made, but he wants the abuse to stop and he figures if that is what is necessary to bring the issue to management's attention, then that is what he'll do. Besides, he figures, since he has the support of his colleagues, it won't be long before upper management realizes they made a terrible mistake in promoting Ron to the position.

It's at this stage that the rumors will have been going around that Ron is a bully, that he's really hard on Steve, that a new manager is needed, that Theresa should be promoted to replace him, and that Steve is filing a grievance. Some rumors will start circulating about all the bad things Ron has done to irritate or hurt people, as well as things he's done to suck up to his superiors.

Ron is told of the grievance and calls his boss, who we'll call Mr. Big. Ron tells Mr. Big that a grievance has been filed against him. Ron tells Mr. Big that he is not surprised, since he's had nothing but problems from Steve since day one. He'll assure Mr. Big that he has done everything he possibly can to please Steve, but that Steve keeps complaining about discrimination and threatening to cause trouble. He'll ask Mr. Big what he can do to be sure that Steve doesn't fly off the handle and make more trouble. He'll mention something about Steve being burned out, and in need of a change.

By contacting his superior, and framing the problem as Steve and presenting a strategy for eliminating the problem, Ron is preparing the chain of command for a specific trajectory to follow—his own actions will not be the problem, he will be the one taking action to address the problem—which is Steve.

So Ron will be told by Mr. Big, just cooperate with the investigation, turn over all your files about Steve, and any emails you've had with him or about him, and we'll take care of it. Ron's assured he's a good manager and got the job because he's qualified. He has nothing to worry about.

At this point, either Steve or Ron can be mobbed. But remember that part about Ron getting the job because he sucked up to upper management? If those rumors were true, think about it. If they were true, then there's a good chance that upper management wasn't looking to fill the managerial slot with the best manager, but with the most agreeable manager. On the other hand, if they weren't true, and management genuinely believed Ron to the best candidate for the job, they aren't too happy with the suggestion that they are facing an allegation, if not a lawsuit, that they discriminated against a woman. Either way, unless Ron had already been marked as a mistake by upper management, Ron will be safe.

Let's suppose the rumors are true—Ron was chosen because he looked like what upper management thought a manager should look like, and he was a suck-up. That means that Ron has been doing what upper management wants all along, so they don't want to replace him with Theresa—she's a wild card. They want him to stay put, where they can control him.

So Mr. Big picks up the phone and calls HR and asks them if there's been a grievance filed against Ron. He's told there has been, but they just got it and haven't taken any steps yet.

That's alright, Mr. Big tells them, just keep me posted. This guy Steve has been making trouble for awhile and we need to nip this in the bud. We've already looked into it and there's nothing to his claim, but do what you have to do and make sure everything is done right, we don't want any trouble. He's already threatening to go to the lawyers and that's the last thing we need. Ron's doing a great job and we want to keep him.

Do you see where this is going? How will the grievance go? How will the investigator's perceive Steve's concerns? Will Ron or Steve become the focus of the investigation?

Now think back to those closed door meetings with coworkers. Who will be called into Ron's or Mr. Big's office? Who will Ron or Mr. Big casually bump into in the halls? And just who is going to get a raise?

If you guessed Theresa, you are right. And who else? Certainly Steve's good buddy, Larry, who he's worked with for years. They even go hunting together and play poker every week.

(And you remember what happened with Larry when he went into that meeting, right?)

Because Steve is alleging discrimination in the workplace, women and minorities will soon receive nice perks, extra resources, plum assignments, and some may even get hefty raises. Talk will begin that there are going to be some big changes, and people will start wondering if those changes will affect their jobs. Might they be out of a job soon? Will there be layoffs? What about new opportunities? Is it true that a new program might be launched with a big budget and they'll need some people to manage it? Steve was the one who spearheaded the push for the program, but he's been so focused on his feud with Ron that he isn't getting his work done. Larry should head it up.

Meanwhile, Steve will be assured by HR that they'll look into the matter and he doesn't need to worry, they'll be fair and objective. They tell him they'll want to talk with him again soon for a more formal interview, but in the meantime, they need a list of his witnesses. Steve leaves, a bit nervous but somewhat relieved, and starts talking to his coworkers who he thinks would make good witnesses. He senses their own nervousness, but that's understandable, and he's confident they'll back him up because that bully Ron has done enough damage.

Phones will be picked up, emails exchanged, people will start talking in the halls and lunchrooms and in afterhours get-togethers. Pretty soon the rumors will shift to gossip about Steve, and how upset he's been. How he's constantly complaining about Ron. How he's so burned out. How it's no wonder Ron's been so short-tempered and hard on Steve. How Theresa would have been a great manager, but she didn't have Ron's close relationship with upper management and the truth is, Ron has really done a good job as manager given what he's had to work with.

Larry, meanwhile, will start feeling uncomfortable around Steve. Every time he sees him, Steve is bitching. First he was bitching about Ron, but now he's bitching about how weird everybody's been. He's becoming completely paranoid, rambling about how everybody is turning against him. No wonder they're staying away. And Steve seems to be obsessed with finding evidence against Ron. He wants everyone to go to HR and help him get rid of Ron. He's trying to manipulate everybody into seeing Ron the way he wants them to see him. Larry really resents being manipulated. And he really resents Steve for making such a big stink out of this. Sure, Ron is a jerk, and yes, Theresa was more qualified. But if he hitches his wagon to Steve at this point, it's only going to hurt him. Why can't Steve just shut up?

Besides, Larry has already talked with Ron, who loved his last report. Ron's not such a bad guy after all.

Little by little, Larry pulls away from Steve. He has excuses for not playing poker, and he's busy at lunch hour. When he does run into Steve, he notices he's really stressed, hasn't been sleeping, is babbling all the time. What a wreck. Steve really should just get a new job. He's burned out.

Steve, meanwhile, hasn't heard a word from HR. He's given them his list of witnesses, but no one he's spoken to has been called by them. It's been six weeks, and nothing's happened. And those six weeks have been long ones. Hardly anyone speaks to him anymore, and at the last staff meeting, everything he said was shot down. His biggest account was transferred to some new guy, and he just found out about a big new project that everyone already seemed to know about but him.

Something seems to be going on, but he can't quite figure it out. People act like they're actually happy, and that's something new. But when he comes along, the conversation stops, the group breaks up, and everyone goes back to their desks.

As for Theresa, she acts like he doesn't even exist—and this whole thing started because he was defending *her*! If he asks anyone for some help or for an opinion or offers to help, it's declined. He's starting to worry. And he's not sleeping. He lies in bed and thinks about everything Ron's done to him that he can show HR to prove he isn't making it up. He never expected it to get this far, but he's beginning to worry that if he doesn't *prove* Ron's been bullying him, that they'll say he made it up. He writes long emails to HR telling in detail what's happening, how a hostile work environment has been created, how he fears that Ron is bribing his witnesses, and at most, he gets curt replies thanking him and assuring him they'll look into the matter.

As the weeks and months pass and his witnesses aren't called and he is increasingly shunned, Steve wonders just what they'll say once they are called. Will they still back him up? He's beginning to have doubts. If HR had spoken to them before Ron got to them, then they would have told the truth. Why did he ever say anything in the first place?

Back at home, things aren't any better. Steve's been irritable and short-tempered, and his wife keeps telling him to withdraw the grievance and just move on. She doesn't understand that it's too late for that. If he withdraws the grievance, he'll be written up for filing a frivolous one. She tries to be supportive, but she has no idea the pressure he's been under . . .

Meanwhile, back at work with Steve a nervous wreck and Ron calmer than he's ever been, the gossip continues about what is wrong with Steve. Even Larry is concerned, and he's one of Steve's best friends. Larry says he's worried about Steve, he says Steve's been drinking too much lately, and that might have something to do with it. Steve needs to get to AA, and to a therapist. Larry's done all he can to help Steve, but there's nothing more he can do. Others feel sorry for Larry. He's right in the middle of it. Steve's obviously trying to manipulate him. Everyone's starting to feel manipulated by Steve. Wasn't he the one who started all this talk about Ron being a bully? If anyone's the bully, it's Steve, for complaining constantly and trying to get them to push his agenda. Theresa didn't even want the job, and besides, she just got a big raise. She says that it was Steve who pushed her to go for the management position, she didn't even want it. Now she says she wishes she'd never listened to him in the first place. He did nothing but use her for his own objectives. It seems the whole workplace has been taken up with Steve's issues, and the sooner he's gone the better—before he does something drastic. Larry said he has guns. . . .

That's how mobbing happens, and that's how rumors shift from sharing relevant information (there's a pattern of discrimination here; women aren't promoted if there is a man for the position; management likes suck-ups; Ron is bullying the staff) to gossip (what's wrong with Steve) to rumors that are neither relevant nor true (Steve's an alcoholic with a gun). And that's when the rumors turn to accusations.

Accusations

If you are mobbed, you will be accused of many things, including crimes and misdemeanors, moral failings and ethical breaches. Management will know that many of these accusations are false, but once management has made the determination you must go, they will do everything possible to make the accusations stick. This is done for several reasons.

The first is that **they want to isolate you from your coworkers and undermine you emotionally**. By smearing your reputation and casting doubt on your character, anything you say will be doubted, and any action you take to defend yourself will be viewed as evidence of your erratic behavior and mental instability, if not an unjust attack on management.

The second reason they will make accusations is because that is the nature of gossip. As we've already discussed, you're eventually going to be cast as a bad person. And bad people do bad things. **In order to make** gossip entertaining, there must be something exciting to share, so it won't take long before someone comes up with something absurd—but still believed by many.

Another reason **accusations will be made is to justify your termination**—this is especially true if you are being retaliated against for engaging in protected behavior, such as reporting discrimination or sexual harassment. **It is against the law to terminate a person for reporting protected behavior. But there is an important exception.** Even if you have filed a claim that falls within protected behavior, if you do something that is so extreme that a reasonable employer would terminate you—such as steal something or threaten violence—*you can be legally terminated.* So if you have reported protected behavior and management is retaliating, expect to be watched very carefully and expect to be accused of theft or of threatening violence (more on that one later—it is probably the most common mobbing tactic).

How do people come to believe these accusations, particularly when they come in the midst of a mobbing? Keep in mind that when you're being mobbed, everyone is at their worst, including you. You will be emotionally flooded and exhausted, paranoid (for good reason), confused, furious, scared, extremely stressed, and getting by on very little sleep.

It's no wonder **people will believe anything they hear about you, because they will have seen you turn from a reasonable, competent worker to an emotionally unstable worker who is barely getting the work done.** As for their experiences in the workplace, other than your issues, they've never had it better. Management's great, warm and friendly, raises and perks are being doled out, and once you're gone there'll be even more money to pass around. So that's one reason they'll believe it.

There's another reason they'll believe anything they hear about you. As Joseph Goebbels taught his own bully of a boss, Adolph Hitler, **if you tell a big enough lie often enough and loud enough, eventually people will believe it.** In fact, we tend to believe big lies more easily than small lies. If we hear something really awful about someone, particularly if it comes from a legitimate and trusted source (such as an employer, co-worker or friend) we may be shocked and find it difficult to believe, but eventually, we'll believe it—or something close to it. It is because the consequences of a grave wrongdoing are so great we're likely to assume that no one would tell such a big lie about someone if there wasn't something to it. We'll err on the side of caution, and presume that where there's smoke there's fire.

Likewise, **if the lie is about something completely contrary to the person's nature or personal values, we may also be more prone to believe it** because shocking as it may be, hypocrisy is something we find titillating. Besides, no one would say such a thing about someone if they didn't have evidence would they? We then reconsider why they were so interested in the subject in the first place. For example, someone who campaigns against child abuse may well be accused of abusing children. Such a lie would undermine them among their peers, alienate them from an issue that is important to them, and be believed by people who begin to question why the accused spent so much time with children.

Another reason **the big lie is readily believed is because it makes us fearful**. It leads us to wonder if we ever really knew the person in the first place, and we begin to think about all the time we've spent with the person never once suspecting they could have done such a thing. The idea that someone we thought we knew was someone completely different can send a shiver up our spine, and even though we doubt the lie, we scrutinize the person for any evidence that we may have been wrong. And when we look for something, we tend to find it.

There is another type of lie that is readily believed, and that is the damning exaggeration. The worker who is known to womanize can easily be accused of sexual harassment, just as the worker who drinks too much can readily be accused of not only alcoholism, but of doing God knows what when drinking. The worker who loses their temper every now and again can easily be cast as a bully, while the worker who is passionate and artistic can be made out to be mentally ill with very little effort.

When Michael Jackson was accused of pedophilia, even though there was little or no physical evidence of such crimes, it was readily believed because he lived in a house called Never Land, had a children's carnival in his front yard, and slept with twelve year old boys. It's not a stretch to pedophilia, yet other than the boys involved, no one in the public knows for sure if he was guilty. Likewise, when Chandra Levy, a young intern for the U.S. House of Representatives, was found murdered Representative Gary Condit immediately became the prime suspect when it was revealed he was having an affair with her. Although her killer was later found to be a serial rapist, Gary Condit's career was over.

In one case, the accusation of pedophilia may or may not have been true but was widely believed because of the unusual behavior of Michael Jackson; in the other case, although the accusation of murder was not at all true, it was enough to destroy a man's career because even though he wasn't a killer, he was proven to be an adulterer—something that probably would have been irrelevant to his career, had the murder accusation never happened. Both accusations of felony behavior were readily believed by the public because the real behavior of each man was morally ambiguous.

Two other types of accusations are likely to surface in a mobbing. The first is **if you have ever done or been accused of anything in the past, it will probably be repeated**. If you have ever lost your temper at some point, you will likely be accused of violence. If you have ever been accused of harassment or bullying, even if exonerated, the accusation will most likely be repeated. If you have ever been fired from a job for cause, that cause may well resurface in the form of a false accusation. Whether guilty or innocent of the past behavior, it will resurface to establish that you are capable of such acts and that you have a pattern of such acts.

The last type of accusation is the type that draws on stereotypes. If you are a person of color, you may well be accused of being lazy. If you are a black man, you are likely to be accused of being violent. If you are a man, you may be accused of sexual harassment, and if a woman, of being sexually inappropriate or falsely accusing someone of sexual harassment or just plain being a bitch. If you are a gay man, you may well be accused of pedophilia. And Lord help you if you're Muslim; you know what they'll start saying, particularly if you're a Muslim male. Stereotypes have a way of worming their way into people's minds without much effort, even if the people who believe them are opposed to stereotypes. They work because we have been socialized to see certain groups of people in certain ways. We may grow to question these stereotypes, but they have entered our minds just the same. **If a mobbing is ignited, so too are our primal fears, making stereotypes particularly effective—just as long as they're couched in "acceptable" language**.

Now that you have a better idea of what to expect when it comes to accusations, you are better prepared for being extra cautious and vigilante, and for not discussing the subject—because to even bring up the subject of any of your vulnerabilities can lead to speculation and distortion.

Going back to our imaginary mobbing, imagine if Steve had confided in Larry that he was drinking too much. What if Steve had invited Larry to go hunting or target practicing? Imagine if Steve had confided to Larry that the workplace stress was affecting his marriage, and his wife wanted him to get counseling.

From Steve's point of view, he would be continuing his friendship with his coworker Larry, confiding in the stress of what he is going through. From Larry's point of view, Steve has told him he has a drinking problem, wants to become a more accurate shot, is breaking up his own marriage and even his wife thinks that he needs help.

The shift from rumor to gossip to more damaging rumors to accusations is one of those slippery slopes that mobbing will put in your path. Be aware of what your own vulnerabilities are, and learn to keep them to yourself. Don't get paranoid, don't start worrying, but do be prepared. And now for what you probably *will* be accused of *no matter who you are or what your work record is*.

You will be accused of doing poor work. Your work product will be judged inadequate no matter how good it is. If it's too good and it isn't possible to judge it as poor quality, it will be considered not what was wanted in the first place, or not original—someone else will get the credit, or you will be suspected of taking someone else's original work. You might be accused of recycling your own work, so that no matter how outstanding it is, it could be judged just a rehashing of what you've done before. Your decisions will be considered poor ones and you will be accused of not producing as much as others (which is usually true, during a mobbing; it is extremely difficult to be productive and think clearly during a mobbing, especially when strategic resources necessary to get your job done have been withheld from you).

You will be accused of lying. Whatever you may have reported or said that started the mobbing will be labeled as a lie. If someone else reported something about you, your defenses will be lies. Anything you say about what is being done to you will be considered a lie, or a product of your paranoia. You will be cast as a chronic liar, someone who has a history of making false accusations, statements or representations.

You will be accused of being mentally unstable. And you will be. Mobbing is crazy making, and you will be at your worse. But you won't just be accused of acting crazy—you will be accused of being mentally ill. Whether it's bipolar, borderline personality, delusional, sociopathic or just plain nuts, expect the label to be hurled and expect it to stick for awhile.

You will be accused of being threatening or of making threats. This is one of those inevitable accusations that enable management to escort you out the door. If you become seriously depressed and possibly suicidal, you will be accused of "making threats of suicide." No one will really give a damn if you genuinely are suicidal, but they'll delight in spreading rumors that you are. Any anger you express will be labeled a threat, and particularly if you are a man, you will be accused of being violent.

You will probably be accused of bullying. This is an easy one, no matter who you are. When you are being mobbed, you are angry at your coworkers and your workplace for how they are treating you. That anger will be labeled bullying. Any complaints you have made or will make about the workplace will be labeled, "constantly complaining." The fact that you are being gossiped about and shunned will be evidence that your co-workers "try to avoid you." Anything you have done in the past such as snapping at someone, correcting them, advising them, or asking them to redo something, will be characterized as "yelling," "insulting," "criticizing," or having impossible standards. The real bullies of the workplace will be excused while your mobbing is going down, but anything you do that can even remotely be described as antisocial, will be called bullying.

The reason you will likely be accused of bullying—even if the incident that provoked the mobbing was your report of someone else's bullying—is because it is a category that is currently widely condemned. **The no toler-ance for bullies mindset that has permeated the workplace, however well intended it may be, has created a universally abhorred category to place unwanted workers**. While it may be difficult to get people to agree to attack *you*, it is not very difficult to get them to agree to attack *bullies*. People are generally not eager to support a workplace policy that says man-agement can retaliate and fire workers who file grievances or complaints, that the workforce should shun coworkers, and that strategic resources, basic rights and human dignity should be denied to workers. But they are likely to agree that bullies should be shunned and fired, that their grievanc-es should not be taken seriously, and that workplace resources, rights and human dignity can rightfully be denied to "bullies" because they disrupt the work place and will not be tolerated.

Once placed in that category of "bully," no one will care what happens to you. "We had to get rid of him," they'll say, "He was a bully."

"Oh . . ."

End of discussion.

There's another thing about the bully label that makes it useful in a mobbing. It's a label. **It's much easier to get people to attack labels than it is to get us to attack people**. So as a mobbing gets under way, name call-ing will start, with "bully" being just one of many. "Difficult employee" is a catch-phrase of abusive management, and as a worker becomes targeted by management, reports will start appearing that describe the target as "difficult." It's a subtle, but significant, shift in how people perceive the person. Official reports will remain professional for the most part, no matter what outlandish conclusions they might come to, or how distorted the descriptions of the employee. Where the real labeling and name calling will take place is among coworkers as their gossip turns catty and juvenile. This is when women become "bitches," men become "S.O.B.'s," "bastards," and "assholes," and the nicknames start.

Labels that stigmatize the target with claims of racism, sexism, and mental illness are especially common, as targets are flippantly referred to as "a racist" who doesn't deserve respect, "an abuser" or "rapist" who should be castrated, a "feminist" who blames men for everything, a "lunatic," "madman," or "sociopath" who should be eliminated. "He" and "she" are commonly used to refer to the person as if italicized, such as comments like "Is *he* going to be there?" "Has *she* gone home yet?" "What does *he* have to bitch about now?" If the person was commonly referred to by first name, they can expect to be referred to by last name. If the person was commonly referred to by a title, they can expect to be referred to by first name. In this way, they are dehumanized—making it easier to be aggressive against them—and disrespected—communicating to the workplace that the speaker has distanced themselves from the person, and no longer respects them.

Shunning and Baiting

Probably the most damaging and hurtful aspect of mobbing—and the least discussed in the literature—is shunning. Humans are social animals; we need the company of other humans for our survival. Again, it's a primate thing—we need each other to survive.

In the 1950's, psychologist Harry Harlow tried saving money by breeding his own monkeys for experimentation. He isolated the monkeys in cages so that they would not be exposed to infection, effectively raising them in absolute isolation from other monkeys. But there was a problem. His monkeys were all severely disturbed—he was breeding crazy monkeys, it turned out.

Introducing them into monkey populations later led to problems with adjustment, and those who had been isolated for one year or more were completely unable to adjust to monkey society and became targets of monkey abuse—like Maestripieri's Macachiavellian monkeys, the other monkeys recognized the isolated monkeys' adjustment problems, and made quick work of their vulnerabilities.

Similar responses have been found among neglected children, orphans raised in isolation from affectionate human contact, and among prisoners. In fact, the damage that social isolation causes is so severe that prisoners and prisoners of war are routinely isolated from other humans as a means to control them and break their will. When Senator John McCain was captured by the North Vietnamese during the war, he was tortured and his arms and legs were broken and re-broken. Yet it was solitary confinement, he said, that was the worst to endure. "It's an awful thing, solitary. It crushes your spirit and weakens your resistance more effectively than any other form of mistreatment" (McCain, quoted in Gawande 2009).

In a New Yorker article on the effects of isolation among humans, Atul Gawande discusses these and other studies of social isolation, noting that EEG patterns on humans who have been isolated for long periods of time suffer measurable changes in their brains lasting months later. The impact of social isolation on the human brain is as severe as if the subject had suffered physical traumatic injury to the brain. Once returned to society, they seek out human contact at every opportunity and talk incessantly, yet suffer difficulty with emotions, sleeping, and eating—pretty much what we see with mobbing targets.

The longer people are isolated, the more likely they will have difficulty initiating and sustaining social interactions, appropriately interpreting verbal and nonverbal cues, and organizing their lives around daily activities and goals. They also become severely depressed and hopeless—again, strikingly similar to how mobbing targets respond in the aftermath of a severe mobbing—and display irrational anger—a hallmark of mobbing targets who lash out with ferocity at the treatment they receive (and in rare cases, they respond with violence[1]). In fact, Gawande notes that research has demonstrated that up to 90% of isolated people react with irrational anger, as compared to 3% of the general population.

Although mobbing targets never endure the total isolation that prisoners may suffer, shunning is a form of social isolation that renders a target effectively isolated from those who once gave their life meaning—and economic sustainability. Shunning is the single most effective tactic to disempower and damage a mobbing target—and one of the easiest to achieve.

As previously explained, people will distance themselves from the mobbing target, and bystanders will join the gossip little by little, transforming themselves to participants in the aggression. Shunning does more to damage and wound the mobbing target than any of the accusations or abuse, because it will communicate that they are unwanted, disliked, and no one cares about what is happening to them—at a time when they need support more than ever. So what will they do? Will they run and cower in their office? Perhaps, but more than likely, they will strive to reach out to their colleagues, while knowing as they do so that they are indeed driving everyone nuts, and that no one really understands what they are going through.

They'll try to get their friends and coworkers to understand. They'll often tell them how stressed they are, not realizing that doing so only gives further fodder to the gossip. They'll tell them what terrible thing has been done by management, thinking they'll realize that no one should be

---

1 I would argue that the single most predictable factor in identifying potential workplace shootings would be a male gun owner who has little or no social support outside the workplace and who is a target of workplace mobbing, shunning, ridicule and/or internal investigations. Ironically, however, rather than cease the abusive treatment that provokes such extreme reactive violence, organizations are more likely to justify intensifying the abuse against such people, rather than diminish it. That is not to say violence is ever acceptable; it is to say that if there is someone in an organization who is targeted for elimination for whatever reason, treating them humanely and fairly at all times may still depress or anger them, but is unlikely to lead to workplace violence.

subjected to such an action—such as monitoring their computer, rifling through their office, taking away their resources and assignments, relocating their office. Unfortunately, that information won't make them sympathetic. It will instead go far to enflame the gossip, as people talk about how crazy, paranoid, and deserving of the managerial treatment the target is. In short, **the more the target tries to get people to understand what they're going through, the more they'll reinforce the view that they deserve it**.

But there will still be people who call, drop by the office or desk or cubicle, maybe even come by their home. These people will want to know what is happening. They'll show concern. They'll ask the mobbing target how they're holding up, if they've seen a therapist, if they've gotten on antidepressants or something, if it's affecting their work. They'll empathize. They'll say that what's happening is so unfair. They'll ask about the latest news. What's happening? What do you plan to do? Do you have evidence? Are you tape recording them? Have you thought about what they might have on you? Have you ever done anything they might find out about? Have you seen a lawyer?

These are the jackals. These are the folks who will take every piece of information they garner, and share it with management and with the gossip circle as fast as they can. This is the stage called baiting. They *want* the mobbing target to babble. They want him to share his rage. They want her to disclose anything and everything. And they'll buy drinks, give hugs, maybe even have them over for dinner.

One reason they won't be recognized as jackals is because they'll be people who once were friends. Remember Larry? By now Larry has kept his distance, but when he does sit down to a beer with Steve, he's thinking in the back of his head, *this guy's a mess, why have I put up with him as long as I have? Why's he telling me all this stuff? It's all he talks about. Doesn't he see he's doing this to himself? I can't wait to get home and tell my wife about the new program I'll be heading.*

We'll get back to Larry later.

Now let's think about who is the bully in this situation. Clearly Steve is not a bully; but it has become the consensus, it appears, that he is one even though that's the complete opposite of what kind of guy Steve really is. The whole mess got started when he objected to Ron bullying him.

But Ron isn't bullying him anymore. In fact, Ron isn't interacting at all with Steve. Nobody else is interacting with Steve, either. And while they snicker when he walks by, exclude him from important meetings and conversations and projects, denigrate his work, and laugh at him every chance they get, how useful would it be if he started complaining that they were *all* bullies? That would only make him look totally nuts. And going after that bully Ron now is the least of his problems; now he's being attacked on all sides, and the gossip and shunning are hurting him way more than the bullying from Ron ever did. Besides, Steve has to ask himself, are they really *all* bullies? Sure Ron is, and maybe one or two of the ringleaders to the gossip circle, but the rest of them were his friends or at the very least friendly coworkers, who never bullied anyone at all.

The cold, hard truth is, Steve is being bullied, but not by bad people. Sure some mean and rotten people are having a field day picking on him, but most of the people who are hurting Steve now are good people. And they believe, genuinely, if not a bit shamefully, that what they are doing is good—they're defending the workplace. When humans become aggressive, we find ways to justify it. We all do it, whether through gossip, punishment, road rage, leaving angry comments on the internet, having a fight with someone we love. We point the finger at them. We justify our own aggression as being caused by someone else. And it's not because we're necessarily bad people. It's because we think of ourselves as good people. And good people don't do cruel things. Unless they absolutely have to. So we tell ourselves we absolutely had to. We had no other choice.

That's how shunning and mobbing happen, and how good people do bad things to people who really don't deserve it.

But how do they come to believe it? How do people actually come to believe some of the things they'll say and eventually even put down in writing? Because by the time the workplace gets done with Steve, he's going to be accused of a whole lot more than bullying. Eventually, his coworkers are going to stop feeling even a little bit ashamed that they exaggerated or even lied about him, because they will actually *remember* he said things he never said and did things he never did.

And that's where Steve has a problem. There is absolutely nothing he can do or say to change all those memories that are about to be created. His coworkers—who are no longer interacting with him—won't remember him as a dedicated and skilled professional they enjoyed working with. They'll remember him as an emotionally disturbed worker who, whatever his qualities, didn't do a good job.

False Memories

When a person is targeted for mobbing, the lies that are told about them begin with your run of the mill he-said/she-said denials and accusations. Ron's being mean, Steve's a troublemaker. As others join in, they selectively incorporate or reject information to conform to what they already believe. That process may initially favor the target, as I've discussed, but once management alerts the workforce to what they want and what cooperating might bring them, they will begin to favor management and select the information that supports that storyline. Then exaggerations, distortions and a few entertaining lies will be tossed around as the group crafts its shared view which will align with management.

But **in later stages, that selective attention will begin to affect actual memories**. Details will be added to the story, details which actually insert themselves into people's memories, the way that eyewitnesses can recall "seeing" a weapon in the hand of an unarmed suspect, or remembering the broken glass at the scene of an accident where no glass was broken. They may even remember experiences they never had.

Nearly one year after an El Al cargo plane crashed into an apartment complex in a suburb of Amsterdam on the afternoon of October 4, 1992, researchers asked community members if they had seen the television film of the crash. Over half reported that they had, and in a follow-up study, two-thirds reported seeing it, recalling vivid details such as the speed and angle of the plane as it hit and a fire before impact. As confident as they were of what they remembered seeing in the televised clip, none had actually seen the film of the jet crashing—because no such film existed.

Those who reported seeing the film weren't consciously lying—they actually "remembered" seeing something they had never seen. Their memories were so clear because they had heard and spoken about it so much that over time their minds filled in the details based on what was reported, and on details they'd seen in photos of the site after the plane had crashed. Another reason they were so confident of their memories was because the researchers themselves suggested that just such a film existed, by asking if they had seen "the" film. By asking the question in a leading manner, listeners subconsciously limited their answers to those which would fit the question.

This is a process known as suggestibility. The language that we use in speaking of an event suggests details about the event which listeners will subconsciously incorporate into their own memories. For example, in a well-known experiment on memory, psychologist Elizabeth Loftus and her associate, John Palmer, showed research subjects pictures of an automobile accident, and then asked them to estimate the speed of the vehicles, using different verbs—hit, smashed, collided, bumped or contacted—to describe the accident, such as "How fast was the car going when it bumped into the other car?" A week later, they were asked if they'd seen any broken glass at the accident scene.

Those who were asked the speed of the vehicles when they smashed into each other, estimated the highest speeds which were reported in descending order, with "contacted" leading to the lowest estimate. Moreover, those who were asked about the vehicles smashing into each other were more likely to "remember" seeing broken glass at the site than those who were asked the question using more passive verbs—despite there being no broken glass at all.

In a more elaborate, if not more stunning, experiment, Loftus and her graduate student, Jacqueline Pickrell, set out to test whether not just details, but entire events could be implanted in people's memories. Twenty-four participants were given a list of four events from their own childhoods (provided by family members), and asked to remember as many details as possible about the events. If they could not recall the event, they were to say they couldn't remember it.

What they were not told, however, was that one of the events they were asked to recall—of having been lost in a shopping mall at the age of 5—had never actually happened to any of them. Nonetheless, one-quarter of the respondents reported remembering the event, and provided detailed recall of their "experience." When told that one of the events had never actually happened, but not told which one, five of the 24 participants reported an event they'd actually experienced as the false one, and believed the false event to have really happened—in other words, 5 of the 6 who "remembered" being lost in a shopping mall, failed to remember real events and continued to believe the shopping mall incident had actually happened to them.

These experiments demonstrate the ease with which memories can be influenced by the manner in which they are presented, and by assumptions we make in our minds about the past. If a group of people are told something happened which never happened, if up to a quarter of those involved "recall" the event—and supply details—it is unlikely that those who don't remember it will insist it never happened. What is more likely is that they will say they don't remember it—and then think back to see whether or not they can remember.

Another feature of memory is that it accords to our social expectations and our stereotypes. We see what we expect to see, something famously demonstrated in 1947, when psychologists Gordon Allport and Joseph Postman conducted an experiment on perception and memory. Subjects were shown a picture depicting several people standing and sitting in a crowded subway. A black man dressed in a suit was talking to a white man, who held a knife in his left hand. After viewing the picture, the subjects described the scene to other subjects, who then told others what was reported, who then told others, for a total of six subjects who had been told about the scene for each person who had seen it. The respondents were from diverse racial and professional backgrounds, and included men and women, adults and children.

In more than half the experiments, a black man was reported to be holding the knife, and in many of the reports, he was reported to be threatening the white man with it or brandishing it wildly. Memories were based on social expectations—what people expected the characters to be doing—not on what the pictures actually depicted—a white man casually holding the knife.

What these experiments tell us is that our memories are not just fallible; many times they're fraudulent. As time passes, we lose recall of details, but when we try to retrieve the memory—such as when we discuss it—our minds try to fill in the missing gaps. We do this by responding to social cues; by recalling details from other events which we apply to the event we're recalling; and by drawing on our biases or expectations of what we *think* we had seen. Sometimes our memories are accurate. And sometimes they're in part or whole just make believe. The problem is, once they become our memories, we can't tell the difference.

So what do all these experiments have to do with mobbing? Keep in mind that mobbing involves rumors to recast a person in a specific light, with potential social and material rewards for helping to justify being mean and cruel to someone, and potential social and material costs for failing to do so. The coworker who "recalls" the mobbing target as having done something to deserve the poor treatment is more likely to be sought after by others for information, more likely to be rewarded by management for helping get rid of "a difficult employee," and more likely to feel confident they are doing the right thing.

Conversely, the coworker who cannot "remember" anything to justify the treatment, or worse, remembers events and details which discredit the disparaging rumors and present the target as a good person and a productive worker, is less likely to be included in the social circle, is more likely to be doubted and dismissed, and can potentially become a mobbing target themselves. Hence, what each participant recalls will have significant benefits and costs, depending on how it conforms to the objective of mobbing.

As memories are revised to conform to social expectations, the rumor mill plays a critical role in the process of recall. Allport and Postman, the psychologists who conducted the crowded subway experiment in the 40's, described how the psychology of recall shapes the content of rumors. They found that as rumors are spread from one person to another, they are transformed through three key processes—leveling, sharpening, and assimilation.

Leveling is the distilling of the rumor into a concise story that is easily recalled. This is the process where details are dropped in the transmission and recall.

Sharpening is the selection of certain details over others as the information is transmitted. Through leveling and sharpening, we tend to forget the details that clutter our story, but retain, reshape or alter certain details which give the story meaning.

Finally, *assimilation* is the distortion of our memories to fit our subconscious desires. This is where the group-think of mobbing leads people to convince not just each other, but themselves, that whatever is being said about the mobbing target is true. It has to be true—everybody's saying it. And soon it is damned true—because they experienced it themselves— even if they never did experience it.

It is little wonder then that mobbing targets find themselves facing an ever-escalating cascade of accusations that begin with vague character indictments, and end with charges filed against them of serious wrong-doing, if not crimes. When leadership openly abuses a subordinate, just like alpha wolves who have tormented one of their own, leadership has signaled to the workforce to do the same. Among wolves, the torment will take the form of bites and exclusion and the stealing of food. Among humans, gossip is the means by which our aggression begins—leading to metaphorical bites and actual exclusion and appropriation of resources.

Given how patterned and predictable the process of social aggression becomes in a mobbing, one would think that targets would be better prepared for what they are up against. But by focusing on good guys and bad guys, bullies and brutes, mobbing targets are inevitably stunned to learn that friends and perfectly decent coworkers have made reports against them, testified against them, and sometimes even filed charges against them—while concurring in unison that "everybody" knows them to be guilty of such awful things—even when such awful things never happened, or at least, never happened in the manner in which they are presented.

But whether they happened or not, the mobbing target is thrust into the bowels of the organization when they must appear before Human Resources, affirmative action offices, internal investigation committees, or even external investigations—such as the EEOC, law enforcement, or the courts. In some cases, these will be investigations the mobbing target has instigated themselves, such as grievances they've filed or claims of discrimination or sexual harassment. But just because they are the ones who called for the investigation does not mean that they are safe. Once a worker steps through the door of an investigator's office, the only safe bet is that the panel will go one of two ways. They will either find *against* the mobbing target, or if they find in favor of the target, *the findings will be ignored* by management. This latter result—finding in favor of someone management wants out—is more likely to occur with external investigations and ad-hoc internal committees comprised of colleagues in other units or departments. Management will persist in finding a legal cause for firing the worker.

Whatever way they go, investigations into wrongdoing are pure hell for anyone to go through, regardless of which end you may be on. But the more you are prepared for them, the more effective they can be in helping to state your case, and in safeguarding you from as much damage as possible.

CHAPTER 5

Investigations and Inquisitions

> There's nothing management hates more than the
> corporate office looking into a problem with one
> employee. When they do, the employee is added to
> the 'kill-at-all cost' list. Every member of management
> will conspire to snag him, even if it does take a while.
> PHIL PORTER, *EAT OR BE EATEN: JUNGLE WARFARE*
> *FOR THE MASTER CORPORATE POLITICIAN.*

Many workers find that when their managers have turned a deaf ear to their complaints, or been the source of their complaints, they go to HR—the Office of Human Resources. After all, that is what they are told to do, having been assured that any problems they might have will be cheerfully resolved by the organization's personnel office.

But that's sort of like being a teenager and assured that if you tell your parents what you really did while they were out of town, they'll be understanding.

They won't be.

Understand two things about HR. The first, which I've already said and you probably already know by now, is that they do not work for you. They work for the organization. They are there to preserve the organization's best interests—as defined by the organization, not by you. They do not report to you, they report to management—which means they comply with the wishes of management.

The second thing to understand, and this is very important, is that if they do look into your problem, they are going to hear many different stories. And each story they hear will come from someone who is absolutely certain of their position. Recall what you learned about memories and perceptions in the previous chapter. As HR looks into the matter, they will hear different perceptions from people who are sincere in their beliefs. If you are being mobbed, those perceptions work against you because lots of people will share the perspective that you are the problem. When someone from HR looks into an employment matter that's transformed into a mobbing targeting you, even if they empathize with you initially, they will eventually hear a different set of facts from so many people that their perception of your credibility is probably going to change.

They're going to believe, and conclude, that you really are a problem.

So the bottom line is, **do not go to HR for anything unless you must. And that means only if you might file a lawsuit and need to show you have exhausted all remedies**. Once you go to HR your problems will either worsen, or your visit will raise a red flag that you are one to watch. If you are sent to HR or do decide to go there, however, be respectful. Do not expect them to do anything to help you. Assure them that you do not want conflict and will do whatever you have to do to reach a resolution to the problem. Keep what you say to a minimum, answer their questions clearly but concisely, and if you still find the problem unresolved, turn elsewhere. That might mean an attorney, it might mean a new job. But do not make HR your sounding board or you will soon regret it.

Sometimes the problem grows beyond HR. When a worker files a formal grievance or report of misconduct, discrimination or sexual harassment, an internal investigation is commenced. In many cases, the worker does not intend for a formal investigation to be conducted. They may merely be alerting a manager to something going on, or requesting the manager have a discussion with the employee in question. But in cases of sexual harassment, managers may be compelled by law to report the incident to an internal unit for investigation. Even when there are policies for first discussing the matter with the worker in question, managers often believe they must report the complaint, so never raise an issue of sexual harassment with a supervisor until and unless you are prepared for it to be investigated.

Unfortunately, as well-meaning as they may be, policies which compel managers to make a formal report and initiate an investigation whenever anyone comes to them with concerns about something that might be sexual harassment or discrimination, preclude any reasonable means of effectively addressing the problem. What they do achieve is a process by which workplace conflicts become formalized inquests which intensify conflicts and destroy reputations and careers. They are rarely objective, rarely properly investigated, and rarely constructive. But they are almost always treated as if they are all three.

Virtually all mobbing targets, except those who leave immediately or soon after the mobbing commences, have been subjected to internal investigations. A mobbing target becomes a subject of investigation through one of two ways. The first is when they bring a problem to management looking for help—what usually becomes "the incident" that sparks the full-blown mobbing. The second is when someone files a report against them. As I've indicated previously, the outcome of such investigations will depend not so much upon facts, as on the institutional power of those involved.

Internal investigations are conducted by Human Resources or Affirmative Action offices or, in some cases, unions or internal ad-hoc committees composed of employees who have been appointed to the committees, but usually have no training in investigative techniques. Even among those in HR or Affirmative Action offices, the investigative training is typically poor. To determine if an investigator knows how to conduct a thorough and impartial investigation, listen carefully to how and what they ask. If they really want to know the facts, and really know how to best elicit them, they will do the following:

- Ensure the witness (which includes the one accused and the one making the report) is comfortable, and knows what to expect;
- Ask non-leading questions;
- Ask open-ended questions as much as possible (to encourage a more detailed answer, rather than yes/no or other short answers);
- Ask follow up questions (which may be yes/no or short answer questions to elicit further detail), and which will include questions such as ""How do you know that?" "What makes you think/say that?" "Can you give an example?" "In what way?" (For example, whenever a person describes speech or behavior with a vague adjective or adverb, such as "He was acting strangely," a trained investigator would always follow up with, "In what way?");
- Will never suggest possible answers, scenarios or examples;
- Will ask who, what, when, where and why questions;
- Will not display judgment in their questioning or interactions with witnesses or display noticeable signs of approval or disapproval when hearing answers;
- Will not assure anyone of what the outcome will be;
- Will not glance at other investigators after hearing an answer, snicker, roll their eyes or make other nonverbal gestures of doubt or disrespect;
- Will contact witnesses promptly, including witnesses who may no longer work in the organization;
- Will not pass judgment about any of the witnesses or individuals involved;
- Will ask witnesses who else might have any information about the matter;

- Will ask the witness if there is anything else they should have asked, or if the witness has anything more to add;
- Will never ask the witness to make a guess for their answer;
- Will not interrupt, unless the person begins rambling or straying off topic;
- Will not rush to fill in silence; the skilled investigator knows that pauses are common, and that more information will be obtained if they wait a moment; the unskilled investigator will be uncomfortable with any silent pauses and will immediately jump to the next question;
- Will avoid negative questions, such as "You didn't do anything to make him say that, did you?" rather than the more effective questions, "Could he have misinterpreted something you said that may have led him to say that?"
- Will not ask judgmental questions, such as "Did you say anything that would encourage him?" A more effective and non-judgmental question would be, "What did you say?"
- Will avoid technical terms or jargon, or otherwise speak over the head or outside the expertise of the witness (yet will not condescend or patronize the witness either);
- Will not reveal information others have provided, except in a very limited manner and only when necessary;
- Will not ask confusing questions with multiple parts; instead they will ask clear and understandable questions, one at a time;
- May express concern about the truthfulness of some of your statements, but will tell you why and will never scold or berate you for your testimony, or suggest that anyone else is lying or making false accusations;
- Will never tell you that you must prove you are telling the truth or your job will be endangered;
- Will never tell you what they have concluded from the investigation so far, and/or what they are hoping you can tell them.

These are the standards for objective and effective interviewing. If you find yourself being interviewed by someone who consistently fails to interview you in line with these standards, then either the interviewer has no idea what they are doing, and/or they have no interest in obtaining the facts. They are interviewing you as a formality and to elicit any information which might be used, or misused, to legitimate the findings they've already decided upon.

Despite the inherent bias of internal investigations, it is likely that if you find yourself brought into the office of an internal investigation there will be a pretense of objectivity and fairness. You will be repeatedly assured that they will be objective and fair, but once you start hearing that reassurance, it's safe to say you won't be. Instead, this is what will happen.

The Internal Investigation Process

If someone else has filed the report of misconduct/discrimination/harassment, either against you or on your behalf, by the time you walk through the door of the organization's affirmative action office, upper management will have been alerted. Recall how this process happens. Your supervisor contacts his or her supervisor, and each in turn contacts their guardians, until the entire managerial hierarchy and a protective umbrella of players have been alerted to be on guard. This communication signals to everyone along the way what is expected of them, so that as the matter is looked into, either formally or informally, and as you seek the intervention of various officials to stop the mobbing, no one will act in accordance with the duties of their office, but all will use their office to rubber-stamp the desired outcome *of their own* supervisor. In other words, they won't try to figure out how to help you. They won't even try to figure out what's going on. They'll focus on how to cover their own ass, which means looking upward for directions on what to do.

If, however, you first enter the investigator's office prior to contacting your own supervisor, the investigators may initially be more open to genuinely listening to your concerns. Once you leave, however, that honeymoon will be over. They will alert their own supervisor, and possibly your manager, that you've walked through their door.

When your manager has learned you have gone over his or her head and filed a complaint and called for an investigation into some sort of conflict, you can prepare for retaliation (it doesn't matter how much you are assured that doing so is against the law; one way or another they will probably retaliate).

Thus, **the status of the manager—not the effectiveness of their managerial skills, but their status in the power hierarchy—will be the primary factor determining how the investigation goes**. If the manager is on some higher manager's shit-list, then the investigation may well turn into an opportunity to eliminate the manager. If not, the investigation is likely to eliminate you—or at the very least, document you as a trouble maker to be eliminated at the next possible opportunity. Don't make the mistake of assuming that just because your manager is ineffective, that upper management wants them to be more effective (and thus respond to your concerns with a constructive resolution). What they want is for lower management to be compliant—to their demands—which is not necessarily effective or responsive to any measly employee's measly concerns.

Once you contact an internal unit charged with investigating these sorts of things, you will be asked to submit a report, outlining your complaint. (In the next chapter, I will tell you more about how to do this.) You will also be asked to attach or submit any supporting evidence (again, more about how to do so in the next chapter), and to provide a list of witnesses who might collaborate your story.

Those witnesses will not be contacted for several weeks, if at all. If you press the matter, you will be firmly told that they are in charge of the investigation and will make the decisions about who to contact and when. By the time any of your witnesses are contacted, their memories will have faded and altered, their perceptions will have been shaped by leadership's communications and expectations, *and you will have become a real drag to be around* because you will have been waiting on pins and needles for the investigation to get started—which as far as you can tell, hasn't happened.

What *has* happened is closed door meetings have commenced, as I've detailed above when supervisors are contacted. At the same time, emails have circulated among administrators and mangers asking what to do, or reporting on what will be done or has been done. You won't know about those emails, but it's useful to know they'll exist, because if you reach the stage of a lawsuit (God help you), you'll want them. But no matter what your intent, the cyber-trail that management will produce will demonstrate that you are a "difficult employee"—even if you became embroiled in the investigation at the request of management.

What has also happened is the investigators have requested your supervisor forward any emails or communications from you, to you, or about you. Management may in turn contact your coworkers, and ask the same of them (once an attorney appears, all coworkers will be notified they are to turn in any and all such communications, which will immediately piss them off and turn them against you, because it will not only take a lot of their time to comply, but will reveal embarrassing things they've said in such emails or communications. The more embarrassing the revelations, the more likely they'll attack you—to mitigate the damage from anything that might be exposed in such emails).

No one will likely tell you they are being asked to turn in their emails.

Your supervisor will be alerted not to discuss the matter with anyone, and your supervisor will then start talking to your coworkers, telling them not to discuss the matter with anyone. (Recall how this is handled, with casual encounters accompanied by praise and hints at good things to come their way, while concerns about you are expressed.)

What no one will be told is exactly what the charges are. What they will be told is that it is under investigation.

Naturally, the more secretive it is and the more they are told not to discuss it, the more people will start to discuss it.

By the time your witnesses, if any, are contacted, and as you already know, they will no longer be in support of you. They will be scared. They will be worn out by you. They will be pissed off at you. And they will have been talking with their boss, with other coworkers, and been listening to the gossip and rumors, and by now you know how that will go.

If any of your witnesses have quit, been fired or otherwise left the place of employment, they will in almost all events, not be contacted (unless it is to defend the organization and discredit you). If your complaint requires demonstrating a pattern of abuse, such as sexual harassment or bullying, other targets may well be hard to find because they will have left, leaving you to look like the only person to ever complain.

In most cases, your employers will begin monitoring your computer, your internet browsing, your emails, and possibly your phone. In some cases, they may even search your office and/or put cameras or recording equipment in your office to monitor you. You will not be told of this monitoring, and it will not extend to others involved. It will be focused on the one targeted for elimination (which for the purposes of this book, we will assume is you, since that is probably why you're reading this book in the first place).

Assume your emails, phone and computer are constantly monitored. Don't be so foolish as to think that you have nothing to hide or that they wouldn't go to all that trouble. It's no trouble for them. It's only trouble for you. Assume they're watching your every move.

Every phone call you make or email you send to the investigators asking the status of your investigation or offering more evidence, will be documented, but probably not followed up, unless it's to assure you that they are looking into the matter and once again falsely assure you that they will treat you fairly.

Other witnesses will be called to testify against you. In most cases, witnesses will have met with management prior to meeting with investigators, and assured that their jobs are not at risk while what they are expected to say has been clearly communicated to them by their managers.

Once they meet with investigators, they will be told that you have made a report, or a report has been made against you, and that they are confident it's unfounded (or founded depending on whose reputation they seek to destroy). The witnesses will be asked leading questions which clearly indicate what they are to say and not to say, and their testimony will be summarized to fit the scenario management has agreed upon.

These summaries will be sent to the witnesses for their signatures, who will in almost every case, sign them no matter how inaccurate they are (but given the fact that by the time the witnesses are contacted, they will have become biased against you, the reports will probably accurately reflect what they said—that you're always complaining and can't be trusted and have mental problems and they never had any problems with anyone but you).

If a witness does object to how their testimony was written up, and points out that the reports and/or interviews were clearly biased and did not reflect what they wanted to say, there is a good chance the report will be destroyed or buried, and the witness's testimony deemed unreliable or inconsistent.

By the time the final results of the investigation are produced, you will have been mobbed, shunned, accused of one to several acts of wrongdoing, possibly demoted, had your work taken away, been professionally and personally disparaged or ignored, received poor performance reviews, been removed from committees, possibly had your office relocated, been deprived of resources necessary to get your work done, and your reputation within the workplace—and possibly beyond it—irreparably damaged.

The findings will be against you, finding either that any and all allegations against you are founded, or any allegations you have made are unfounded.

Then you'll appeal, and your appeal will be denied. If there is an internal ad-hoc committee comprised of other employees in different units who have been appointed to investigate such matters, you may very well have an entirely different experience, and the findings may well support you. But in most cases, such findings will be ignored.

You will be demoted, permanently shunned, and/or fired.

And then accused of even more.

If you find this summary of the process a bit too cynical, step through the doors of HR or an affirmative action office and watch and listen closely to those who conduct the investigation. Are they following the standards of an effective and impartial investigation as outlined above? Keep in mind I didn't ask if they are on your side. I asked if they are following the standards of objective investigative techniques.

They may be decent people. They may be kind and even smart and empathetic and sincerely believe they are doing a good job. But everyone they meet with is certain that they are telling the truth, and the truth they are telling is likely to conform to whatever management wants them to say. Which is to say, if you are the one identified as "the difficult employee," the folks in HR and affirmative action offices are seeing lots of people who are confirming that you are indeed a pain in the ass. And quite frankly, that's probably what you've become in your desperate effort to be treated humanely. So that's how they're likely to see your complain—as an over-reaction by a pain-in-the-ass.

More importantly, they are unlikely to be trained to be the "fact-finders" they'll assure you that they are—and which they believe them-selves to be.

They are trained to help the organization's leadership comply with the law. Not to *make* leadership comply with the law, but to help them to do so—while leadership does whatever it is that they intend to do—which is get rid of the difficult employee.

And when they don't comply with the law, the EEOC and/or the law-yers may step in.

And that's when things get ugly.

EEOC Investigations

The EEOC (U.S. Equal Employment Opportunity Commission) is a fed-eral agency that investigates workplace violations of federal laws, such as

Title VII claims, which are those that fall under the umbrella of a "protected class." That means discrimination based on race, nationality, gender, religion, pregnancy, sexuality and genetic information (which means you cannot be requested or compelled to provide genetic information for employment purposes, nor discriminated against due to you or your family's genetic information, such as being a carrier of a specific trait; nor can they request a family medical history as a condition of employment). The EEOC also investigates complaints of sexual harassment, and of retaliation based on reporting discrimination or sexual harassment.

Two other federal laws protect workers and are investigated by the EEOC, and those are complaints filed under the Age Discrimination in Employment Act (ADEA), and the Americans with Disabilities Act (ADA).

If you do not belong to a protected class, were you discriminated against because of your actions on the part of the protected class? For example, if you are white but raised complaints about how people of color are discriminated against in your workplace, you would still be protected under Title VII.

The EEOC does not investigate complaints of discrimination based on political views because that is not a protected class. If you are a conservative and almost everyone else at work is a liberal, they really can fire you just for watching Fox News. (But chances are they'll mob you first, so read on.)

The EEOC does not investigate complaints of being fired for tattoos, piercings, hot pink hair, or lip plugs. If you want to look like a psychedelic pin-cushion with Smurf-colored hair and have a fiberglass Frisbee inserted into your lower lip, go for it. Just know that your employer doesn't have to go for it.

And the EEOC does not investigate complaints of discrimination for private (non-governmental) employers of less than 15 workers (for Title VII or ADA claims) or 20 workers (for ADEA claims).

It also does not investigate complaints of bullying or mobbing—unless they are related to your protected status. That is because *it is not against the law to bully or mob anyone.* We'll get to other remedies later, but for now, let's focus on the EEOC and when and why and how to file complaints with them (and when and why not to do so).

As inept and biased as some of these internal investigations may be, you cannot file a complaint with the EEOC or the courts until you have exhausted all internal remedies for relief. What that means is that before you can turn to the EEOC or file a lawsuit, you must demonstrate that you have followed your organization's grievance procedures and cooperated with their investigations, and that no corrective action has been taken. In other words, you have to show that you did everything you could to seek help, and they didn't do anything to help you.

What the organization has to show when you do so, is that they did indeed respond to your concerns. They don't have to show that they found in your favor; they just have to show that they conducted an adequate investigation and followed their own rules. They also have to show that they have complied with the law, but in many cases, that means they just have to insist that they did so—as in, "Of course we didn't discriminate; read our mission statement—we're all for diversity and inclusion; they're just a difficult employee."

Just as you cannot file with the EEOC until you've shown that you have followed internal policies and procedures first, you cannot file a lawsuit in federal courts for discrimination based on protected status until you have filed an EEOC claim and received what they call a "Right to Sue" letter. This document essentially says they've looked into the matter, and have either found reasonable or probable cause for your complaint, or no cause. No cause does not necessarily mean no cause to sue; you can still sue, but depending on the reasons for the no cause finding, you just might have a more difficult time finding a lawyer to take your case.

In other words, *before you can sue in federal court, you need the EEOC to do its thing, if your suit would be related to an act protected by one of the federal employment statutes* (Title VII, ADEA, ADA). (You may sue in civil court without going through the EEOC, but I'll get to that later. For the time being, let's focus on violations of federal laws—your civil rights.)

In about five percent of the cases they investigate, the EEOC will file a lawsuit on your behalf, but that is usually only in extreme cases, and usually only involving discrimination against a large class of employees and involving a big employer.

Regardless, once you get a Right to Sue letter from the EEOC, it compels you to act quickly or forfeit your claim. We'll also get to that later. First, a few points about the EEOC investigative process.

The investigators at the EEOC are overwhelmed and understaffed. A lot of what they investigate is absolute nonsense. They have no end of complaints filed by angry and hysterical people who can't tell the difference between discrimination and their own incompetence. Others may well have been discriminated against, but the damages they have suffered are relatively insignificant (but their problems often become significant once they've filed). And some complaints that EEOC investigators handle are so serious and reflect such long-standing and pervasive patterns of discrimination, with serious abuse of workers, that other complaints of discriminatory treatment look mild in comparison.

Add to the overwhelming workload the fact that they've had staff cuts of up to 25% in recent years—just when the economy tanked and workplace discrimination escalated by 15% (as minorities and women become the first to be laid off by some employers)—and you can appreciate just how challenging it is for investigators to effectively and efficiently get through their case load. They're overworked and burned out, and your complaint is just one of hundreds that will cross your investigator's desk— and that means you're going to have to wait a long time for anyone to look at your case, and even longer for anyone to do anything.

And what they will do is not likely to make you happy. They are not going to punish anybody. They are not going to get you any damages. What they are going to try to do is look at your case as fairly and as quickly as they can, and if they find that it has merit, they will require your employer to try to resolve the matter with you, through a process of mandatory conciliation. The EEOC does not seek damages; it seeks corrective action.

But by the time they get to the point of seeking corrective action, the problem will probably have either resolved itself, or gotten so out of hand that no corrective action is even possible. Even if you would absolutely love corrective action, if you are being mobbed in your workplace, corrective action is the last thing your employer is interested in. Had your employer given a damn about corrective action, someone in management would have stepped in long before and nipped the mobbing in the bud. If they didn't do so, it is because they support the mobbing—they want you out and nothing you can say or do will change that view. They do not want "your" problem corrected. Rightly or wrongly, they view *you* as the problem that needs correcting.

So they aren't going to pay any attention to the EEOC.

What that means for you is that if you think the EEOC is going to be a solution to your problem, you're wrong. EEOC investigators may well be sympathetic, but filing with the EEOC is likely to lead to further animosity at work, be an extremely frustrating process that drags on for up to a year or more, and lead to few if any improvements in your life or work. But if you think you may have to sue your employer (another losing battle, but sometimes necessary), then you will have to file with the EEOC. If so, go into it with your eyes wide open.

How you file makes a difference. When the investigators begin to look into your complaint, they will be unimpressed by emotional venting, sobbing, rage, or panic. They will be unimpressed by a litany of everything your boss ever did that was unfair or heartless—which may well be a long list. And they will be unimpressed by complaints you have been bullied—unless you can clearly tie that bullying to your membership in a protected class.

At this point, you should consult an attorney. Even if you cannot afford an attorney, if you reach the point where you are going to file a complaint with the EEOC, you should recognize that you are on the path to a lawsuit—your costs are going to sky-rocket, and the cost of an attorney to help file the EEOC complaint are minimal in comparison to what you will incur if and when a lawsuit is filed.

The more fact-based and void of emotion your complaint with the EEOC is, the more sane and thoughtful you will appear. You have the right not to use an attorney, but if you are in the midst of a mobbing, chances are you are overwhelmed emotionally. If you cannot afford an attorney to file it for you, consider having a trusted friend (totally unassociated with the workplace) or family member help you file it. You do not want to bury the EEOC investigators in an avalanche of "proof," but you do want to outline the actions and adverse actions that were taken, the dates, and any statistics or data you might have to support any claims of discrimination at your place of employment.

The first thing the EEOC will do once they get your complaint is determine whether to rank your complaint as Track A, B or C. Track A means there is a reasonable cause to believe a violation has occurred. Track B means your complaint needs further investigation. And Track C means there is no reasonable cause for your complaint and they will not investigate it.

If the EEOC investigator ranks your complaint as Track A or B, they will request a Position Statement from your employer. Your employer will deny your claims. They will counter that you have always been a problem and they have bent over backwards to accommodate you. You will then be given the opportunity to reply to their claims.

When you do so, again, restrain the emotion. Respond with exact dates, specific actions, and any supporting data or evidence you may have. In other words, "show, don't tell." The investigators will be more convinced of your position if they are able to review your evidence and come to their own conclusions, than if you merely insist that you've been wronged.

You may be encouraged to provide signed Affidavits from coworkers about your treatment. If you can obtain such Affidavits, it might be very helpful. But chances are, it will be the opposite. Asking your coworkers to sign anything opposing their employer—no matter how much they might be chomping at the bit to do so—is risky. Chances are you will alienate them by asking them to stick their neck out like that, and if you persist, they will turn against you with a vengeance. If someone offers to provide you a signed statement, great, but it's unlikely anyone will. Don't pressure anyone to help you; when you go against an employer, you're pretty much on your own, so get used to it. But also know that the EEOC investigators will be talking with coworkers (if they get around to an investigation), and when they do, they'll have a good sense of what's going on—unless you've alienated your coworkers in the meantime (in the next chapter, I'll explain how to limit that alienation; it's a certainty, but there are also many things you can do, and not do, to minimize the mobbing.)

The EEOC will also ask you to consider voluntary mediation. This is a non-binding procedure which encourages you to sit down with your employer to reach a constructive resolution. You have the right to an attorney or advocate in the mediation process; by all means, do whatever you can to find and hire an attorney. Few advocates are knowledgeable about employment law, and if they are affiliated with an organization working on bullying or the workplace, they're own interests will influence how they advise you—which is very often wrong. For example, you might find an advocate with an anti-bully organization who assures you that you deserve a hefty settlement. But their idea of what you deserve will not necessarily be based on the law, on your actual damages, or on how your case is likely to be valued by the EEOC and/or a jury. They could very well damage your case by their own claims, so be wary of advocates.

If you enter mediation, do so knowing that the best you can hope for is probably a neutral recommendation and a mediocre severance package that is worth less than your CEO's cufflinks. The EEOC investigators are not friends of your employer. But that doesn't automatically make them your friend either. They are looking for clear and compelling complaints of *specific* actions taken against you by your employer which are related to your membership in a protected class and/or which suggest a violation of your civil rights. It is up to you to demonstrate that your employer took an *adverse action* against you due to your membership in, or association with, a protected class, or in retaliation for reporting a protected action.

And it had better be a clear and demonstrable adverse action. Don't run to the EEOC if your employer said you had to start coming to work on time or criticized your work product or treated you rudely. An adverse action means you were fired or demoted, had your salary cut, were passed up for a promotion you were objectively qualified for (in favor of someone outside the protected class with significantly fewer qualifications) or took some other action against you that other employees outside the protected class were not subjected to.

How are other members of the protected status treated? If you are a woman in a primarily male workplace and you were not promoted to a position for which you are qualified, while a man was, you may have been discriminated against based on your gender. But if your employer can show that other women have been promoted, even if not at the same rate as men, you will have a difficult time demonstrating discrimination. Moreover, even if you can show that the women who were promoted were buxom sex kittens who slept with the boss to get their raises and promotions, that does not necessarily mean you can prove discrimination. It means that you will have a more difficult time proving discrimination.

Once your employer has taken an adverse action against you, you have 180 to 300 days (depending on which state you're in) to file with the EEOC. This is a critical deadline—if you miss it, the EEOC will not investigate your claim, and *you will not be able to sue under the federal statutes* (you might still have a suit in civil courts, but that is something only an attorney can advise you on).

Be careful how you interpret an adverse action. For example, let's say you are a Hispanic man born and raised in Texas and you are up for a promotion for which you are clearly qualified, and you have been assured that the job is yours. But someone at work doesn't want you to have the job, and tells people you're an immigrant who is taking jobs from others and someone anonymously starts sending anti-immigrant jokes and videos around to your coworkers. You file a report with the affirmative action office, they promise they'll look into it, and then nothing comes of it but a report that says the other person denied making the racist comments, and there was no evidence of who sent the videos and jokes. In fact, they conclude, you may have sent them yourself to get attention and sympathetic support for your promotion.

Shortly after the report comes out, you are passed over for the promotion in favor of a non-Hispanic white woman who is far less qualified than you. You have 180 days to file your complaint, but at first you have no interest in going that route. Instead, you start to grumble to your coworkers about how minorities are treated in the organization, and once the woman who was promoted over you takes her seat in the manager's chair and becomes your new supervisor, it becomes pretty clear she doesn't like you.

After awhile, you find that you're being criticized constantly, your work load is doubled and your resources are slashed, and your office is moved to the far side of the moon. So you go to the Affirmative Action office and file another complaint. Your supervisor, the woman who was promoted over you, counters that you are constantly complaining, you are not getting your work done, you're haranguing your coworkers, and you have been repeatedly warned that you have to shape up or you'll be fired.

You turn to your coworkers for some support, but instead they begin to shun and mob you, and before you know it, you're accused of using your office computer for personal use (who doesn't?), bullying people into going along with your claims of discrimination (you're just talking to them, trying to get them to stop taking it and do something about it), and finally, of stealing office equipment (you took an office laptop home to do some afterhours work, just like you always do; you even told the secretary you were taking it and it's not your fault she didn't write it down and now says you never told her). You finally reach the end of your rope and you tell one of your coworkers that you just saw your boss in the parking lot while you were pulling into work and you resisted the urge to run over the bitch.

And that's when you get fired—for stealing and threatening your boss—and you are escorted out of the workplace, carrying your box of personal items as the police escort you to your car. You are humiliated and enraged. Now you're going to file that EEOC claim, you decide. Now you have a whole list of adverse actions.

But guess what? The only adverse action that you can tie directly to reporting discrimination was the initial act of passing you up for a promotion—which happened seven months earlier—one month past the 180 day deadline. That adverse action doesn't mean you actually were discriminated against; it means that you *may* have been. Nonetheless, the fact that you can show a *possible* link means that adverse action could have been investigated under Title VII. But now it's too late. You missed your opportunity.

But what about all those other actions, you ask? So what if you missed the 180 day deadline about being passed up for the promotion. What about all the accusations, what about doubling your workload, what about moving your office to Outer Mongolia, what about firing you unfairly?

Those other acts were related to your bitching and grumbling when you should have been working they'll say. Your manager will argue that whether or not you were discriminated against, you began bullying your coworkers, and you broke the law by stealing and threatening your employer. Those are legitimate reasons to terminate you. **The federal courts have ruled that firing an employee for a legitimate reason—even if that employee has reported protected action and cannot lawfully be retaliated against—is legal if any reasonable employer would have done so**. And that means if your employer can show you were stealing, not doing your work, or engaging in violence or threats of violence, they can legally fire you—even after you have filed a complaint with the EEOC.

If this should happen and you are accused of something that merits your dismissal, and you eventually file a lawsuit, your attorney will try to argue that the other actions against you were a pretext—in other words, trumped up to make a case for lawful termination based on discrimination. You may have suffered additional adverse actions which you can show were retaliation for making a report, but if you never filed an internal complaint or grievance about discrimination when it first happened, you'll be hard pressed to make your case—even if you're right and you were discriminated against. You might prevail, but the chances of your case getting thrown out for not meeting the deadline of the initial cause of action are high. So to best preserve your legal claims, you must do the following:

- Exercise all internal remedies; and
- File your claim with the EEOC within your state's statutory limits (180 to 300 days) from the date of the *initial* adverse action.

If you fail to file within the statutory limits, but additional adverse actions are taken, you may still have a case, but with every subsequent adverse action, chances are greater that your employer will be able to argue that it was for a legitimate reason and unrelated to your protected status. Only an attorney can analyze the facts of your case and advise you of your options. The bottom line is, *cover your ass by filing within the statutory limits of the first adverse action, because if they are indeed discriminating against you, they will seek to terminate you for a lawful reason*—which means they will encourage your coworkers to watch your every move, they will be taking notes of every mistake you make no matter how trivial, they will try to catch you stealing something, they will monitor your emails and computer and possibly phone lines, and they will push you to the breaking point—in hopes you'll make a threat.

Ultimately, the EEOC will find that there is either probable cause or no probable cause to your claim. If they find probable cause, you must make an effort at mandatory reconciliation. That means sitting down with your employers and trying to reach an acceptable resolution. An acceptable resolution from their perspective will be that you go—no matter how unfair it is and no matter how great a hardship—at the least possible cost to them.

No matter how much you may want to stay, leaving is as much in your best interest as theirs, because once you've been marked as a "difficult employee" and mobbed, your status is permanently handicapped. Recall the animal kingdom. Like Bridget, the wolf that spent her life with her nose hanging down and her tail between her legs, your place in the organization has been relegated to the trash heap. If you must stay (which is sometimes the case, particularly for older employees), you will gain self respect by building a life outside the organization. But if at all possible, leave with as much money and self respect as possible.

And if that's not possible—probably because all they offered was a fistful of coins tossed at your feet—then get real. Either you don't have a case or your employers genuinely don't care (or both). So if mandatory conciliation fails, and it probably will or your employer would have resolved the matter long before, the EEOC will either prosecute your case for you (again, something they do only in rare cases and usually only involving multiple claimants), or they will issue you a Right to Sue letter. And then you will have 90 days to file a federal lawsuit.

Another possibility is that the EEOC will find no probable cause to your claim. Don't be alarmed if this happens. In almost all cases they investigate, the EEOC finds no probable cause. That is because if they were not able to investigate the matter in a timely manner, which they probably couldn't do because they're so overworked and understaffed, they will issue a no probable cause finding. The only difference between probable cause and no probable cause is if it's the latter, you do not have to go through the reconciliation process before filing a lawsuit. You still have only 90 days to sue from the time you receive the EEOC finding, however, so don't delay—if that is what you decide to do.

Lawyers and Lawsuits

There's a saying among employment lawyers that the minute you file a lawsuit against an employer, you've already lost. It's that bad. But before it even gets to that point, you have to find a lawyer. And before you start looking, know this: your employer will not be intimidated by your lawyer. Your employer will lawyer up and let their lawyers take over. And that means war.

Once a lawyer contacts your employer on your behalf, all employees will immediately be alerted not to speak about your case to you or anybody. And that means that they are not to talk to you about acting as your witness or providing any statements. It means if they haven't already shunned you, they will start doing so. And it means that your employer will begin talking with your coworkers about the testimony they have against you—this is the time when all employees are expected to team up with the boss and demonstrate that they are team players, loyal to the organization. Those "small betrayals" that came earlier in the casual meetings with your boss and coworkers, will now blossom into full-scale attacks against you.

Your coworkers will also be alerted that they are to turn over any and all emails to you, from you, or about you, as well as any other correspondence you have shared. And as I've said previously, not only is that very inconvenient, but it exposes their own gossip and badmouthing to their bosses. They will be furious with you—and the more that they have to turn over to the bosses will embarrass them, the greater their aggression against you will be—to not only punish you but to mitigate any damage they might suffer from whatever the contents of those emails reveal. The fastest way to mend a damaged relationship with the boss you once referred to as a fascist asshole in an email, is to help that boss gun down the person that you sent it to—the one now suing your employer.

So **it's usually not a good idea to hire a lawyer just to scare the employer into behaving. That's likely to backfire**. But there are still good reasons to consult an attorney. An attorney can tell you whether you have a case against your employer or not. In many instances, employees who have been wronged and treated badly are stunned to discover they have no legal cause of action against their employer. It's not against the law for your employer to treat you like crap, scream at you, insult you publicly, and heap a ton of work on you at the last minute. Just as long as your employer treats everybody badly, they're off the hook.

They're also off the hook if they treat only people with red hair badly, or only people who dress in polyester. Just as long as they do not discriminate based on membership in a protected class, they are not legally liable.

But they may still be sued if they breach your contract or otherwise violate civil or federal laws. There are a number of civil causes of action which may pertain to your case, and they include not just breach of contract, but slander, libel, civil conspiracy and others. The only effective way you can know if you have a civil claim against your employer, is to consult one or more attorneys—which means finding an attorney, presenting your case to the attorney, and considering what steps you would like the attorney to take.

First, be sure you look for an employment lawyer who specializes in representing plaintiffs. Check your local (county and state) bar associations for lawyer referrals, and/or Google "employment lawyers." Then review the website. Read the "About Us" section. If they say they do defense work, it means they represent the employers. They defend against cases like yours. While they might sometimes take a plaintiff's case, chances are they won't be interested in yours because it won't be as lucrative as those hourly fees, and if they do take your case, they can never represent your employer because they'd have a conflict of interest. An employment lawyer specializing in defense does not want to burn bridges with any employers in the community. So find an employment lawyer who represents plaintiffs.

Second, read over the attorney bio's. Where did they go to law school? What types of cases have they tried? What kinds of settlements have they received (if posted). Do they take *pro bono* work? That means service for free, and many attorneys devote a certain number of hours each year to *pro bono* work. Unless you are utterly broke and you have a compelling case, however, chances are you'll have to tap the savings account, pull out your credit card, or take out a home equity loan to pay for legal advice.

Do not assume your lawyer will take your case for a contingency fee. Attorneys only take cases on contingency if they are willing to go to court. No attorney worth a damn is going to agree to a contingency fee on an out-of-court settlement that does not involve a formal lawsuit. To get to the point of a hefty settlement, they will have to file a lawsuit, and as you'll learn in a few minutes, once filed, what follows is pretty much out of your control and drags on for ages. So just know, if you consult an attorney about a workplace issue, you are probably going to have to pay some money up front, at least in the early stages.

Third, go to the county and state bar association websites and check if there have been any professional actions taken against the attorney, such as a suspension, rebuke, or disbarment. It's not likely that there have been, but it's always possible. It happened to me. I'd hired an attorney only to discover that his license had been suspended—a fact he failed to mention. Fortunately, I discovered the suspension in time to stop payment on the hefty check I'd written him. Google the attorney's name and see what comes up. Avoid attorneys who have been sued multiple times, faced ethics inquiries, or are notorious ambulance chasers.

It's also a good idea to avoid friends and family, unless they specialize in employment law. They might be good for behind the scenes advice and minor things, but if it looks like you may be heading to court, find someone who specializes in employment law.

Finally, many attorneys now request that you submit your queries via their website. They tell you to concisely state the facts of your case and an attorney will get back to you. *Be careful!* At this point, you do not know whether they have a conflict of interest or not. The bigger your employer and/or the smaller your town, the greater the chances that someone in their firm has worked for the employer, is married to someone who works for them, or has represented some of their employees who are now witnesses against you. **Until you know for certain that there is no conflict of interest, anything you tell a potential attorney, however "confidential" it should be, can potentially get back to them**.

So if you're filling out one of those website forms just write, "I work for Company X and have a potential discrimination action against them. I do not want to discuss the facts of the case over the internet. Do you have a conflict of interest that would prevent you from representing me? If not, may I consult with you by phone or in person about my case?" If you call a law office, present your case in the same basic way—don't reveal the facts of your case or the strategies you are contemplating over the telephone, until you are confident there is no conflict of interest.

If the attorneys do have a potential conflict of interest, you have revealed very little. If they don't, the attorney(s) will know that you are rational, cautious, and have a potential case. They will probably agree to meet with you—but before you do, be sure you are clear on whether or not the consultation is free (it usually is, though the meeting will be from ½ to 1 hour and no more), or if there is a fee.

When you meet with the attorney, do not bring all your evidence. Do not ramble. Do not rage. Even if doing all three is what comes naturally—you are most likely devastated, furious and scared if you've gotten that far, and if you are being mobbed, you're all the more scared and mad and wounded. But you must be prepared.

Bring with you any EEOC or internal reports you may have filed, any final investigative reports, and any employment contracts you have. If there are some specific documents related to your case, such as a termination notice or a clear communication of discriminatory treatment (such as a memo declaring a new hiring policy that workers over forty will not be interviewed, or an email telling you if you hadn't reported the discriminating treatment, you would have been promoted, but because you had, you will no longer be considered for the promotion). If the attorney agrees to represent you, there will be plenty of opportunities to show him or her all your evidence, but for the initial meeting, keep the evidence focused and selective.

Be sure you know the key dates of your hiring, firing, and other relevant decisions pertaining to your employment status. The attorney will want to know when deadlines and statutes of limitation are coming up, so have a clear timeline written down that shows when you were hired, when you were promoted, when adverse decisions were made, etc.

Be clear about what you want. The attorney will evaluate whether or not you have a potential legal case, and will want to know what you want to do. If you have no legal case or don't want to go that route, an attorney may still be able to negotiate a respectable severance package for you. If you do have a legal case, your attorney can help you decide whether or not you should file a claim with the EEOC, file a federal or civil lawsuit, or take other action.

Be wary of the lawyer who is chomping at the bit to file a lawsuit, who assures you that you'll make a lot of money, or who guarantees you any particular outcome. Nothing can be guaranteed other than more conflict.

And do get a second and third opinion. Doing so will give you a much better insight into whether or not the legal advice you are receiving is reasonable or not. Do not go with the attorney who promises you the most. Go with the attorney who advises you the most realistically.

Unless there is a statutory deadline looming to file a lawsuit, or you are preparing to leave your employment and want to negotiate a severance package, **the best course of action is to have an attorney remain in the background**. Have your attorney advise you, help you file any internal or external claims, review communications or otherwise guide you, without appearing publicly. That means do not have your attorney write a letter to your employer saying you are now under legal representation. Do not have your attorney file any documents under his or her name. Simply have your attorney advise you behind the scenes—which is what your employer's lawyers are doing.

If the problem still persists, and you decide you want to file a lawsuit, be forewarned. It's going to be a whole lot harder on you than it is on them. Your boss and coworkers will go about their lives pretty much uninterrupted except for the occasional testimony they might have to give or meeting about what to do about you. But they won't lie awake at night worried about how they'll survive without a paycheck. That's your problem.

And your bosses and coworkers probably won't have to turn over their medical records, their mental health records, be compelled to take mental health exams, and have all their former employers told what a problem they've been and asked about problems anyone's had with them. That's all going to happen to you, but it's not going to happen to them.

Your bosses and coworkers won't have to explain to anybody about why they should be hired and why the problem with you ended so badly— you're going to have to be looking for a job and interviewing and explaining what went wrong, but they're not. They're busy working.

And your bosses and coworkers probably won't have forensic teams comb through their computers, review all their emails (including the deleted ones) and check out every website they ever visited. That's likely to happen to you, but not to them.

In other words, the lawsuit is your burden, not theirs.

And a lawsuit is not going to divide and conquer them, if that's what you're thinking. It's going to unite them. They will unite against you, just as you find yourself isolated from those who once were your allies.

The litigation process opens up a whole new can of worms that turns mobbing into a legal lynch mob. Once you file a lawsuit, your conflict with your employer becomes a public record which anyone can look at. It also exposes you to the laws of discovery, which means they can and will ask for your medical and mental health records (if you claim personal injury or emotional stress), your past employment records, your computer hard drives (sometimes even your home computer hard drives), any employer-owned cell phones, past addresses (so they can interview former neighbors), and the names and contact numbers of everyone you have ever discussed your job or employer with.

Moreover, **contrary to what most people think, lawsuits don't usually lead to speedy settlements. Once filed, they drag on**. If they do not lead to a rapid settlement when they are initially filed (and they usually don't, because in most cases the employer is given the opportunity to settle before filing), then there are two times when they are most likely to settle: right after deposition—which may be one to two years after filing—or right before trial—which may be two to four years after filing. And if you think those years will fly by, you're wrong. They might fly by for your employers and coworkers, but the attacks against you will persist day in and day out without let up and in public for as long as you are involved in a lawsuit. And remember: their attorneys are paid hourly. It's in their best interest to drag it out for years.

A lawsuit is so damaging to a plaintiff that it is best left for those who have no hope of recovering otherwise, who are unlikely to find other work, and who have exhausted every possible remedy. For the most part, **if you are under fifty, you're probably better off not suing, no matter how illegal or cruel your employer's actions**.

Filing a lawsuit will not make you whole. It will not bring you applause. It will not bring you justice. It will not vindicate you. But it will expose you to incredible abuse, publicize your workplace problems for all the world to see, and it will go on for years—years in which you could be focusing on new work and growing in a new career.

If you must file a lawsuit, however, do so knowing what's up ahead. If you are being mobbed now, understand that a lawsuit will only make the mobbing much, much worse. **Run, don't walk, from a potential lawsuit if there's any chance of finding another job**. You may suffer a huge blow to your income, you may have to move, but you will recover much faster if you get out of a toxic workplace as fast as possible, and do not end up battling in the courts no matter how egregious your employer's actions may have been. A lawyer may be able to help you negotiate an exit, however, so by all means consult with an employment attorney, but preferably toward a peaceable resolution. But because your employer won't give a damn about peace-making with you, understand that whatever that resolution may be, you'll probably get screwed. But better to get screwed than raped, and that's what's up ahead if you file a lawsuit.

So now that I've disenchanted you of justice, just what can you do if you're being mobbed or bullied? In the next section, I'll give you some tips on how to stop it, or at the very least survive it.

PART II

How to Stop (or at Least Survive) Mobbing

How to Stop (or At Least Survive) Mobbing

Of all the many things you can and should do to survive a mobbing, there are three things you can do which will be damned hard, but will do more than anything else to help you to survive. These three things are: **control your thinking; control your emotions; and grow up.** Now before you start sending me hate mail, listen up. There is a reason you need to grow up: mobbing is a devastating attack on your identity and humanity, and because it is so devastating, it will rapidly reduce you to tears. It will take you back to an emotional state of childhood when the bullies were picking on you. It will make you want your mother. It will leave you feeling powerless. And now more than ever, you need power. So you need to calm the child within you, and muster up the grownup that you are.

There's another reason you need to grow up. You are at war. It's time to be a man, even if you're a woman. This is a test of what you're made of.

And there's a third reason you need to grow up. Most of what we complain about at work is really pointless. Most of the grave injustices and abuses we suffer are really better off ignored—or stored in a file of our minds labeled "useful information."

Now I know that sounds flippant and insensitive, but let me tell you—as someone who lost way, way more than I ever thought possible to lose—when I look back on what I was so upset about at work, I snicker. I snicker because had I simply ignored the small injustices, I never would have endured the great ones. If I had laughed off the bad behaviors, I never would have suffered the atrocities. And had I left my ego at home when I went to work, I never would have had it slaughtered by the people I worked with and trusted.

It doesn't mean I deserved it. It doesn't mean they were right to do it. And it doesn't mean it is okay by any means. What it means is that I walked straight into a den of alpha wolves and offered up my jugular, when I should have just kept my mouth shut and observed them.

In short, mobbing forced me to grow up in ways I never would have understood before or during my mobbing. But now that I am past it, I can provide a more objective take on what leads to mobbing. And what I've learned is that in so many cases, mobbing turns into a wildfire of torment because the person who has been targeted has let their mind run in an endless loop of wrongs they think need to be righted, cannot control their emotional wounds and rage, and they have put their egos ahead of their interests—which is completely disempowering.

That doesn't mean they aren't good people—many targets have a high sense of ethics and their complaints do have merit. (Unlike some anti-bullying experts, however, I'm not going to tell you all targets are good and all targets have superior ethics—rotten no good scoundrels with the ethics of a lobbyist can and do get mobbed. And so do decent, hard-working ethical people. Anyone can be mobbed.)

Maturity requires learning how to control how and what we think, how and what we feel, and what we say and how we say it. It also means weighing our options not based on idealism, but on reality. And the reality is that pursuing justice is usually a lonely pursuit, and one that offers little reward. We need justice in our world, and we need idealists. But don't put your career on the line for your ideals (nor sell out your ideals for your career). There are other ways to fight for fairness. But when it comes to the injustice in our own worlds, far too many mobbing targets find themselves blinded and buried in their pursuit for justice. And once blinded and buried, we cannot effectively achieve any meaningful victory over injustice.

What almost all any mobbing target wants is really not a lot. Mobbing targets want the abuse to stop. They want to work. And they want an apology. That's all. But as simple and reasonable as those three things are, they are not going to come at all once a mobbing commences. So what mobbing targets must do is protect themselves.

There are three ways in which you must protect yourself from mobbing. You must protect yourself emotionally, socially and professionally. By doing so, and by learning to control your thinking and your emotions and by acting from a place of maturity, rather than neediness, you'll go far toward managing the mob. So listen up and toughen up, because in the next three chapters I'm going to tell you what you need to do if you're going to survive the mob.

CHAPTER 6

Protect Yourself Emotionally

t's all about your emotions. You're feeling terribly hurt, crushed and devastated. You're furious in a way you've never known before. You feel true hatred for the first time ever. You're terrified, scared and distracted. You don't know what's coming next.

In a word, you're emotionally overwhelmed. But before a mobbing target can effectively respond to the shunning and onslaught of personal and professional attacks, he or she must control the emotional flooding that mobbing produces. There are four reasons why it is imperative that to do so.

First, emotional flooding can be deadly. Anytime we are emotionally overwhelmed, we are prone to stress-related illnesses. It is not unusual for mobbing targets to suffer heart attacks or strokes or develop cancer shortly after being mobbed. Many are made to feel so worthless and unwanted that they commit suicide. Others, such as former LAPD officer Christopher Dorner who went on a murderous rampage in the wake of his termination from the police force, have been known to kill their coworkers, managers and others in a desperate effort to gain power over a situation which has left them feeling utterly powerless. The documentary, *Murder by Proxy*, is an excellent exploration of the role mobbing plays in many workplace shootings, and how some may have been avoidable had the targets been treated more humanely.

Second, emotional flooding confuses us, making it difficult to concentrate and get our work done. When our coworkers and managers are out to get us, becoming an unproductive worker is hardly in our best interest. A mobbing target must work extra hard to avoid any perception they cannot do their job, and do it well.

Third, it is impossible to effectively respond to aggressive attacks and escape the mob (by getting a new job, for example), if you do not have control of your emotions. At the very time you have been made to feel completely worthless and loathed and utterly crazy, you must muster the poise, confidence, and control to respond to repeated accusations of misconduct, find a new job, and perhaps even pursue a lawsuit. It requires the strength and emotional control of a Navy SEAL to respond to mobbing, so there's no more critical time to gain control of your emotions than when they are understandably exploding inside of you.

And **finally, anyone who is emotionally overwhelmed is a drag to be around**—the mobbing target almost always finds themselves alienating their support system at the time they need it most because they are constantly babbling about how awful their situation is and how furious and depressed they are. No one can withstand hearing that for very long before they're ready to run for their lives from the pitiful friend they wish that they could help but would rather just escape. If you're being mobbed, chances are your friends and family are feeling overwhelmed themselves; give them a break from your emotions by gaining control of them.

To control your emotional flooding, understand that there are three primary emotions that mobbing provokes: anger, fear and sadness. Each of these emotions is experienced as a range of feelings. Unchecked anger turns to fury and rage; unchecked fear turns to paranoia; and untreated sadness turns to anguish and serious depression. All of these emotions are normal and natural responses to threats to our survival, but they become maladaptive when they are not controlled. To control the painful feelings associated with mobbing, here are a few steps you can take to gain greater control of your emotions when you are under group attack.

Control Your Thinking As I said earlier, no one ever says, "The more I thought about it, the less important it became." The more we think about anything, the bigger it becomes in our minds, so **we must first control our thoughts before we can control our emotions**. Every time we think about an emotionally-provocative event, we relive it. Our brain does not distinguish between the real event and the memory of the event, or even the fantasy of the event.

When intrusive thoughts enter your mind, it is imperative to break the cycle. Creating a verbal command, such as "No!," "Stop!," "Get Out!" or any other short but forceful command, accompanied by a visual image of kicking, pushing, or blowing the thought right out of your head, will eventually—*if repeated consistently*—interrupt the repetitive thinking that causes mobbing targets to fume and relive the attacks. Control your thoughts, no matter how justified and accurate your thoughts might be.

Diminish the Power of the Thoughts Closely aligned with intrusive thinking is the *power* that we give to the thoughts that enter our minds. To counter this power, every time an angry or fearful thought enters your mind, cripple it with absurdity. Choose an utterly ridiculous nonsensical sound, word or sentence to silently scream to yourself the moment a powerful but negative thought enters your mind. The more ridiculous, the better, because the idea is to abruptly cut off the thought before it takes form, and shift the mind from the serious to the silly. What that does is interrupt the neural pathways that repetitive thinking creates, shifting the active parts of your brain from your amygdale—where anxiety takes form—to the lower frontal lobe—where humor, judgment and decision-making take form.

It will require constant repetition before it is effective, but if every time you think about how much you hate your attackers, you instantly scream to yourself something silly and meaningless, like "Squally Giggle Pickle Juice," the hatred will lose its power—and so, too, will your attackers. It does not mean that the attacks are silly—far from it—but it means that you have the ability to control your responses to the attacks, and therefore, a greater chance to survive them.

Seek Calm The most important thing you can do to protect yourself emotionally is to control the constant chatter in your head that is enflaming your pain and rage. It's not easy when you are being mobbed because every day can bring a fresh assault that stuns and crushes you. But with practice, it becomes easier, so be sure to apply the techniques previously discussed about interrupting the repetitious and negative thoughts that are eating you away. Another step toward this end is to surround yourself with calm.

Try turning off the news (unless you find it distracts you from thoughts of the mobbing). Instead of listening to NPR on your way home from work, listen to a CD of ocean waves, classical music, or a spoken word inspirational CD. Don't play rock or pop music at home, even if you love it. It will stimulate you, when what you need at this time in your life is calm. Play relaxing music, surround yourself with relaxing scents and soft lights, take warm baths.

If you have kids and returning home means a whirlwind of activity, do your best to immerse yourself in that activity because it can help focus you on something far more important than your work. But as the stress becomes too much, find a sacred space in your home where you can be at peace. If there's no such space, go for a walk, go to a movie, head to the spa (even if you're a man who thinks spas are only for women—they're not; one gentleman's facial and you'll thank me). The important thing is to reduce the noise in your head and your home and replace it with peace and calm.

Focus on Your Body Mobbing takes a huge physical toll on a target, and as our bodies are weakened, our minds all too often follow. That means you need to exercise, no matter how much you'd rather not. Join a gym, take up running, martial arts or ballroom dancing, but *get yourself moving.* Focus on strength training, to feel emotionally stronger. If you begin to feel depressed, move. Stand up, check your posture to be sure it is erect, walk, even if you only walk across the room (avoid walking to the refrigerator; overeating won't help!). But by moving our bodies, our minds and sense of self will follow.

Similarly, pay attention to your diet. Overeating or not eating are both high risks you'll face if you're being mobbed. Pile the vegetables on your plate, reduce the carbohydrates, increase the protein, and avoid junk food. Watch what you drink and if you're hitting the bottle a bit too heavily, stop altogether, at least for as long as you are under attack. A drunken brain and mouth is the last thing you need right now. One drunken email or phone call could tank your career. If you're drinking, sober up.

Focus on Your Physiology When we become aroused, our bodies enter the "flight or fight" mode and respond physiologically. Our faces and/ or ears redden, our hands shake, our mouths snarl or slacken in defeat, our fists clench, our postures become rigid, and we begin to sweat. By paying attention to our personal physiological responses, we can learn to control them, and the emotions and thoughts that trigger them. Techniques that help slow our heartbeats and respiration include biofeedback, meditation, exercise (again!), and humor. Control your physiology and you can better control your emotions—and you won't look like the wounded wolf with its head hung low and its tail between its legs that everybody wants to pick on.

Seek Laughter I can't stress enough how important humor is to surviving any trauma. Immerse yourself in comedy, in small and larger doses. Take continual breaks to watch three minute YouTube video clips of standup comedy (but not on your computer at work), listen to Pandora's comedy station, watch old sitcoms, new comedies, read funny books. Seek out humor everywhere, and do it often.

Shift the Emotion When an emotion is overtaking you, identify the emotion (I'm angry, I'm sad, I'm scared, I'm confused, etc.) and ask, What do I want to feel? Happy, secure, at peace, etc. Then ask yourself, what is one *small* thing that I can do to get there? The key thing is that the step is a small one—anything big is not likely to happen, and it becomes just one more damned thing you have to do at a time you're overwhelmed. But a small thing might be to watch that three minute funny video, wash the dishes, put on your favorite shirt, walk the dog. But do it. And know that it alone is not likely to change your emotions. But it is a small shift, and if done again, and again, it can begin to shift your emotions and give you a greater sense of control than if you simply let your emotions simmer on their own.

Check Your Meds If you are taking any psychotropic medication, especially anything for attention deficit disorder, it may intensify your anxiety. Check with your doctor and if at all possible, do not take any medication that has side effects of anxiety, agitation, rage, depression or suicidal thoughts. If you must take it, talk to your physician about tapering you off or changing the medication. You may benefit from anti-depressants or anti-anxiety medication, but again, check with your physician and remember that having a bottle of tranquilizers on hand is not a good idea if you are feeling at all suicidal. If you live in a state where medical marijuana is legal, and you are comfortable taking it, that may be the safest form of medicating your anxiety, but if you are heading for litigation and/or subjected to drug testing, it may work against you. In my view, medication side effects are one of the greatest threats to mobbing targets, and one of the least discussed, because medication has the potential to turn a seriously stressful event into a calamity for the target whose brain is chemically altered. (Add to that the fact that half the people mobbing you are probably on psychoactive medications themselves, and you can just imagine how aggressive and irrational the situation can rapidly become.) And as stated previously, if you drink, be sure you are not drinking too much. Even the most moderate drinker can find themselves self-medicating with alcohol when they are being mobbed.

Avoid Writing About It You're going to need to write some things down, particularly if you find yourself in litigation or internal investigations. But sending long-winded emails, engaging in anti-bullying forums or blogs that encourage being angry, are usually not helpful.

Every time you write down what has happened to you and how you feel about it, you give the event greater power and you emotionally relive the attack. (And anything you write online can and will be discovered and used against you.) Record what is necessary for your legal strategy, as I discuss subsequently, but otherwise do your best to avoid writing about your experiences and what was done to you, until you are at an emotional and physical distance from the mob. Writing about it will probably not diminish your anger, fear or sadness, but it will increase it. Some people advocate journal writing as a form of release and for some people, it is. If you are prone to writing, by all means, write about it in a private setting. But not until you are in an emotionally and professionally safe space for doing so—and if you are heading for a lawsuit, be aware you will be required to turn over your journal to the opposing side—so if you do journal, do so cautiously. And if at any point you find it stimulates your anger and/or anguish, stop journaling until the abuse has stopped.

Engage in Role Play This is a powerful technique to help you deal with hateful people. If you continue to show up to work as yourself, you are likely to expose all your vulnerabilities—all your pain, all your rage, and all your paranoia. Don't let them see it. If you are falling apart, send someone else in your place—and in theirs. Would Hilary Clinton wilt at the scorn from these nitwits? Hardly. Imagine you are Hilary and channel her in your every stride and smile. You don't even need to like her to find her power useful. Or perhaps Oprah can give your presentation, Clint Eastwood attend the meeting, or Bart Simpson join the gang for that sexual harassment lecture (just as long as he keeps his mouth shut).

Find a role model to take your place—or multiple role models—who exhibit grace under pressure, confidence, power or just plain fun. Play a character, and play it all the way. From the way you stand to the way you dress (within reason!), to the thoughts inside your head. What would the Dalai Lama do? What would Walt Whitman be thinking about their opinions of him? What would Michelle Obama or Jacqueline Onassis say in this situation? (Avoid channeling characters like Dorothy Parker or Darth Vader; they'll only get you in more trouble.)

Playing a character enables you to draw on qualities inside yourself that have been pummeled by the abuse you're suffering, without having to second guess yourself or react in patterned ways. If you are a woman working in a largely male environment, perhaps you can play the role of a confident, successful man. Use fewer words, speak more slowly, and don't focus on your emotions. These might be very difficult mannerisms for *you* to master—but much easier for your character to exhibit. If you are a man, you might find playing the role of a woman helps you to feel more compassionate, creative or beautiful. These are stereotypes, yes, but sometimes stereotypes can be useful. For whatever qualities you want to bring out in yourself to better face the mob, find a character or characters you can play that will help you to do so.

Study the character—the way s/he/it walks, holds their head, uses their hands, and sets their mouth. How do they dress? How do they live? What kind of environment do they create in the rooms they live in? Think of the many roles the Merrill Streep has played, from Julia Child to Margaret Thatcher. In each one, she draws on an entirely new set of emotions and mannerisms to become that person. How does Dustin Hoffman succeed in convincing us he is an autistic man in one film and an assertive woman in another? He lives the character, in every nuance and thought while he is playing the role. Learn from these masters of method acting, and you'll find it far easier to get through the social onslaught of the mob than you can do just by being yourself when under fire.

At the same time, find replacements for those who are causing you so much pain. If someone makes you burn with rage at the very sight of them, replace them with a ridiculous image—maybe Baby Huey, that giant diapered cartoon character sucking a pacifier. When you see the person you so deeply resent, immediately think to yourself, Baby Huey. Imagine tears springing from his face. Every time. Eventually, the sound of his name or the sight of his face will instantly bring Baby Huey to your mind, and what could be more silly? Or what about that backstabbing coworker you thought was a friend and is now suddenly the darling of your bully boss and has spread hateful gossip about you to justify her bad behavior? Don't imagine her as Wicked Witch or Elvira the powerful vamp. Imagine her as a dust bunny, a squirrel or a potted plant. Give her a role that has no power, can do no real harm, and is not worth thinking much about. Then her enhancing power will appear more ludicrous and pathetic as you increasingly come to associate her with something that is, ultimately, insignificant.

Substituting one association for another is powerful *if you do it repetitively and consistently.* It is a particularly useful technique for fear, and when you are being mobbed, you have good reason to fear public encounters with those who think badly of you. To be most effective, imagine as many details as you can when you evoke the substitution—the smell of the diaper, the dirt of the dust bunny, the wilting leaves of the potted plant. Evoking such details brings the image to life, and makes it more believable.

Find Yourself a Mental Muse Another helpful technique in role playing is to give yourself a muse or a mentor, or even an imaginary friend. Just as children create imaginary friends to help them cope with loneliness or abuse, Christians find courage and comfort in the knowledge that God is always at their side, or ancient Greeks called on one of nine muses for protection from calamity, you, too, can create your own protector from your imagination or your faith.

Think of someone or something that puts you totally at ease, whether it's a childhood playmate, a giant teddy bear, or a wise old shaman who you can conjure to be at your side at any moment. Don't shy away from the goofy or ridiculous—a bit of levity can go a long way. If you have a deceased parent, ancestor or friend who you always turned to in times of trouble, conjure their spirit—it isn't necessary that you genuinely believe in ghosts or Gods or imaginary friends—to the extent that you do, great, but even if you don't, there is power in imagining they are there. Use the power of your imagination to make them real.

Take your muse or imaginary friend along whenever you encounter the mob. No one but you has to know. To help in this effort, you may find it useful to have a totem—a symbol or emblem of the spirit that protects you. Perhaps you will keep a small charm of an eagle in your pocket to remind you that the eagle soars higher than any bird, and catching sight of an eagle is a sign that your prayers have been heard by God. Perhaps a white feather, a smooth stone, or a photo of a religious figure can bring you a sense of peace and power just by touching or seeing it.

Converse with your muse, allow it to counsel you as you encounter emotionally difficult situations, and *allow it to shoulder your burden for you.* Keeping your muse by your side will help you to feel supported and not alone, especially at times you feel most alone.

Learn Something New As trite as it sounds, learning something new can really help. The idea is to put yourself into a situation that forces you to concentrate on the task at hand and to be present in the immediate moment. What happens when you are being mobbed is that you constantly think about all the many things that have happened to you, and all the many things that could happen to you. You live in a constant state of fear, teetering on the edge of the uncertain future and the painful past. When you think about the past you are crushed and enraged and when you think about the future you are terrified. What's going to happen? What will they do next? What could you do to them next? What if you lose your job (you probably will)? How will you pay the rent or mortgage, much less support your children? How will you find a new job at your age and with all those horrible things being said about you?

It's impossible to be present in the immediate moment if you are constantly thinking about what has happened and will happen. You need to focus on the present. And a useful way to do that is to learn a new skill which requires your focus. In many cases, you will not be ready to learn many new skills. If you are being mobbed, it's no time to take up brain surgery. But by drawing on your existing skills, talents and interests, but taking them to a more challenging level, you can find yourself quickly immersed in something other than the thing that is hurting you so much—and you might even find you have a new, marketable skill that could land you a new job.

For example, if you love to cook, learn a new cooking technique that you haven't previously tackled. If you're a painter, try another medium, such as sculpting or photography, something that draws on your artistic talents, but requires you to pay close attention and learn something new. If you like to golf, consider learning to play tennis. If you love technology, learn a new one (resist the urge to take up hacking your employer's computers, however tempting it may be).

Whatever it is that you tackle, don't make it too easy—you don't want to find yourself so settled in your comfort zone that you are operating automatically, allowing your brain to wander and intrusive thoughts to assault you. But don't make it too drastic a change either—your brain isn't quite up to par and you don't want to set yourself up for failure because you decided that you'd like to learn to sew when you've never threaded a needle and have no patience for accurate measurements. Start with something you love and enjoy doing, and ask yourself what you could do to take it to another level. Then do it.

Do Not Embrace an Identity as a Victim When you are a victim of abuse, it's hard not to feel like a victim, especially when part of surviving the abuse means recognizing that you are a victim. But if you want to recover, you will need to first accept responsibility for your role in the conflict. You need to take a good, hard look at yourself and ask yourself how you have escalated the conflict. Many anti-bullying experts will tell you that there is nothing you did to bring it on. But that is a terribly disempowering message to embrace. It suggests that there is nothing you can do to slow or stop the abuse. You cannot change the behavior of the people mobbing you. You can only change your own behaviors—which in turn, may well affect theirs.

Carefully reflect on your emotional reactions and displays. Are you allowing your anger or pain to be seen? Are you venting and accusing in your responses to the myriad reports and "findings" and accusations that will come your way? It's normal and natural to do so, but because the people who are attacking you have convinced themselves that they are acting appropriately and for the good of the workplace—and that you deserve it—they will consistently counter all your claims with even more hurtful claims of their own. Look closely at how your own actions and reactions have produced fears and furies among your coworkers. Don't be harsh on yourself or on them at this point. **The idea is to be observant and come to see the ways in which how you act and react contributes to how they act and react. Doing so won't make you guilty or responsible for their actions. It will empower you to become better able to control what they do to you.**

When you begin to see yourself as an actor in the conflict, rather than a victim, you will grow stronger. More importantly, the more you view yourself as a victim of bullying or mobbing, the more you solidify that role as your permanent identity. Mobbing entails a crippling revision of your identity—people are characterizing you as incompetent, unstable, unethical, and untrustworthy. They are shredding your personal, social and professional worth and redefining you to fit their image. This is no time to embrace a new identity as a victim. You are someone who made some bad choices and as a result found yourself the target of someone else's aggression, and that person or people fostered a climate of collective aggression against you. You may have been victimized by them, you most certainly were targeted by them, but you do not need to spend the rest of your life as their victim. Empower yourself by taking responsibility for your role in the conflict, and refusing to define yourself by this single, horrible episode in your life—even if it ultimately strips you of your financial and professional security as it did to me. There's so much more to you and your life than what they did to you. Do not embrace the identity of victim; embrace your identity as victor by becoming stronger, calmer and wiser.

Meditate Whether you're a practicing Buddhist, a Fundamentalist Christian or an atheist, meditation can help. There are many forms of meditation, including contemplative prayer, and all help you to learn how to be in the present, shed the anxiety and worries of your past or coming day, and put the mind into a state of calm. That is something that you'll need when you are under attack. You need calm. And you need to *not* think, and to just be. Meditation does that. It focuses the brain inward, but without the clutter of mind-chatter that only riles you up.

The National Institute of Health has found that meditation can change neurological processes in the brain with beneficial results. A number of scientific studies have shown it can increase concentration, improve academic performance and memory, and even improve self-control and reactions (Hölzel, et al. 2011). Meditation is particularly effective for alleviating stress and anxiety and depression .

Don't be resistant to meditation just because it sounds like hocus-pocus or is too New Agey for your tastes. Meditation has been practiced for centuries and by all major religions. It's effective, and that's what you need right now—something to help reduce your stress and get you out of your own confused mind.

Focus on Gratitude Like the suggestion to "learn something new," being thankful for what you have sounds hokey. But it works. Whether you start a journal of gratitude, practice prayer, or simply think through all your blessings at the end of the day, the more you can focus on all the wonderful things in your life and in your day, the more you will find yourself shifting from the negative mindset that mobbing produces, to an optimistic mindset that makes room for joy.

No matter how much the mobbing may have taken from you, there are always far more blessings in your life that you still have—and far more to come. Moreover, as mobbing accelerates, it takes even more from you. If you still have a paycheck coming in, no matter how paltry, be thankful. You may soon be without one. If you can breathe, be thankful for the health you do have. If you aren't homeless, be thankful. Whatever you are suffering or whatever you have lost, others have lost far more and would give anything to trade places with you. Focus on what you have in your life to be thankful for.

Similarly, at the end of each day, and preferably throughout the day, reflect on everything that brings you joy, comfort, hope, confidence or humor. Whether it's something as small as a smile from a stranger, a funny movie that took you out of your pain for a couple of hours, or an opportunity that has come your way, spend a few moments to think about it. Actually think about it, and recall how good it made you feel, if only for a moment. Relive that good feeling in the same way that thinking about all the bad things forces you to relive those bad emotions. Remember, at the neurological level your brain can't distinguish between something that is happening to you, and something that you remember happening to you. You will relive the emotions you felt when something first happened every time you recall it. By forcing yourself to think about the good things that are happening to you as they happen, and to recall them at the end of the day and remember how you felt when they happened, you will relive those good emotions. You deserve to.

Seek Counseling Last, but not least, get professional help. But be careful. Some mental health practitioners do more harm than good. You want someone who is good, who understands mobbing, and will not encourage you to rage at your attackers, view yourself as a victim, or tell you that you did nothing to bring it on. If that's the kind of a counselor you want, you can just have Siri, the robot voice on your iPhone, tell you all those things.

If you are being mobbed, it is important that whatever counselor you find understand something about group psychology. If they don't understand mobbing or group psychology, even if they understand something about workplace bullying, you could find yourself being diagnosed as paranoid once you start telling them about how many people are indeed out to get you.

If you do find a counselor who you want to work with, but they don't understand mobbing, bring them something (brief) to read about it so that they understand that people really are out to get you, and that you are up against not just individual bullies, but the dynamic of group psychology. A useful article is "Workplace Mobbing: Are They Really Out to Get Your Patient?" published in 2009 in the journal, *Current Psychiatry*. This article, written by psychiatrist James Randolph Hillard, discusses how he almost institutionalized a patient for paranoid delusions, until he learned about workplace mobbing. (You should be able to find the article online with a quick Google.)

Another type of counselor that is probably not helpful while you're being mobbed is one who will want to go into detail about your childhood and parents. You probably will benefit by exploring your past and how you have responded to social conflicts, but a counselor who prioritizes psychoanalysis or other forms of long-term psychotherapy will not be a good choice for dealing with the immediate trauma and emotional flooding of mobbing.

Counselors who are skilled at diagnosing and treating PTSD (Post-Traumatic Stress Disorder), using cognitive treatments which focus on your thinking patterns, and/or biofeedback (to alleviate stress through physiological control), and multi-modal approaches (using a variety of techniques) are probably going to be more effective in helping you to cope during a mobbing than those who want to get at the childhood or prenatal roots of your trauma. Hypnosis and possibly acupuncture may also be effective, but avoid psychics unless you're just looking for a shot of goofy. They are ill-equipped to provide effective advice to someone facing something as serious as a collective mobbing.

One last word of caution, and that's using Employee Assistance Programs (EAP) counselors. These are counselors who have contracted with your employer to provide counseling to its employees. Many are fair, objective and effective, but far too many are concerned with alienating a source of their income—for these counselors, a mobbed worker may be viewed as a potential threat to their own relationship with the employer because they may have to produce a report about you and possibly be called as a witness. If you must see an EAP counselor, be cautious with what you reveal until and unless you are confident that they understand

and recognize the impact of mobbing, and won't view your sessions as a mandate to document how crazy you are.

For all potential counselors, be sure to ask if they have any conflict of interest with your employer, and be careful to distinguish between those who are defensive of the employer, and those who are merely trying to help you view the problem more objectively and holistically. The former are more likely to perpetuate and reinforce the image of you as the problem, and may even breach your confidence by communicating with your employer about your sessions, whereas the latter will be more concerned with helping you to heal and to maintain your ability to think clearly and reduce your anger.

Controlling emotional flooding does not mean that there is no reason to feel the emotion—when under collective attack, there is every reason to be furious, depressed and afraid. But before you can effectively respond to, much less survive mobbing, you must be able to control your emotional responses. Start with controlling your thinking, follow by controlling your body, and you will find yourself gaining greater emotional control to survive the painful wounds of workplace mobbing. It's not the only solution, but it is a critical one for anyone under collective attack. Because mobbing is a collective attack, a lot of people are going to turn against you. You will need to limit the number who do turn against you, minimize the intensity of their aggression, and preserve your social support when you need it the most. In the next chapter I'll suggest a number of strategies you can take to help you survive socially.

CHAPTER 7

Protect Yourself Socially

> Sometimes paranoia is just having all the facts.
> WILLIAM S. BURROUGHS

B y the time you realize you're being mobbed, a lot of damage has already been done. Recall the closed door meetings that will have gone down once an "incident" puts you in the line of fire. If there has been an investigation, many of your coworkers may have already been speaking with HR and the Affirmative Action office, if not the EEOC if you have filed with them. Don't assume they'll tell you about these meetings. They probably will not (there's also a good chance they've been instructed not to tell you).

Even if there has been no identifiable incident and you haven't (yet) been accused of anything formally, or filed a report against someone yourself, if the shunning has commenced, your evaluations have suddenly taken a nosedive, and the resources necessary to do your work have been shrinking noticeably, you're best advised to protect yourself from further social damage. **Remember, the emotional pain and professional damage you suffer from a mobbing are directly related to the social damage that is inflicted. Manage the social damage, and the emotional and professional fallout will be significantly lessened**.

Expand your social network outside your job and profession. One of the reasons that mobbing is so terribly painful is because humans tend to rely on other people to validate our purpose in life. When the people we work and spend so much time with turn against us, we truly are not valued. It isn't just a matter of not *feeling* valued—if you are being mobbed you have received a strong message that your value to the organization and your coworkers is so unwanted that they are willing to devote great resources to being rid of you and will publicly defend their views as legitimate—regardless of what you have previously contributed to the organization or your relationships, regardless of your potential to contribute in the future, and regardless of the consequences you and your family suffer. And that's a harsh message to receive, no matter how unjust. It is devastating.

Psychological research has demonstrated that regardless of a person's personality, if they are ostracized for even a few minutes by total strangers, they will feel the pain acutely and make efforts to be noticed (Williams 2001). In a workplace setting, where you have developed personal relationships with the people who ostracize you, and where being ostracized can have severe economic ramifications as your job and career are threatened, the pain is extreme—literally. When a person is ostracized a part of the brain called the dorsal anterior cingulate cortex is stimulated—the very same part of the brain that registers physical pain (in fact, some research suggests that the social pain of ostracism can be diminished by taking acetaminophen or Tylenol because the brain does not distinguish social pain from physical pain [Randles, et al. 2013]).

Because ostracism is so painful, humans will go to great lengths to avoid it. According to Kipling Williams, a psychologist at Purdue who studies ostracism, being ostracized psychologically impacts us by threatening four fundamental human needs. It affects our sense of belonging, our self-esteem or sense of self worth, our sense of control over our lives, and our sense of having a meaningful existence. When all four of those needs are kicked out from under us simultaneously, it is very difficult to muster up the capacity to respond in a healthy and effective manner, but that is exactly what you need to do if you are going to make it through the gauntlet of workplace ostracism.

Consequently, when you are involved in a conflict against an employer, it is very important to establish new relationships in other social circles, and to revitalize others that you may have neglected, just so long as they are unrelated to your employment or profession.

It is common, however, for mobbing targets to put almost all their energy into trying to become reintegrated with the group that is excluding them. They feel that the most important support they can receive when under attack from an employer is the support of their coworkers who can legitimate their concerns about the workplace and/or how they are being treated.

But once you realize that your coworkers are humans acting at their worse in the maelstrom of a mobbing, you will realize that seeking their support will only put you at greater risk. As you now know, your coworkers will have been courted, discretely and behind closed doors, by your employers. You have learned that those closest to you will have been courted and seduced by management, encouraged to make "small betrayals" and been slowly turned against you.

By pressuring them to support you, especially if they are close to you, if they are members of your same protected status relevant to your claim (such as other women if you've filed a sexual harassment claim, other people of color if you've filed a discrimination claim), or if they are publicly committed to diversity, strong labor laws, or social justice—qualities that suggest they *should* recognize the injustice you are fighting—you are more likely to anger them, than you are to gain their support.

That is because they may well feel they ought to be on your side, but doing so exposes them to potential abuse themselves, and going against you might very well benefit them. Rather than feel bad about themselves for not doing more, or for not having the courage to stand up for their own ideals, they will psychologically go to great lengths to see *you* as the problem. As others are doing the same and gossip against you swells, going against you is made that much easier.

So muster all the compassion you have inside you and try to see that they are scared, and when people are scared they usually do one of three things. They freeze, run away, or attack. They do not run toward the person who is being burned alive. So where does that leave you? It leaves you vulnerable (and burning alive). And it leaves them freezing (bystanders who do nothing to help); running away (shunning); or attacking—you. Don't chase after them and don't appeal to them for help or understanding, no matter how desperately you want both.

Be especially careful to keep your distance from those who will feel the greatest moral conflict in holding or extending their support. And if they are potential witnesses on your behalf, let others, such as your attorney or EEOC investigators, appeal to them. You stay out of it. If you get your social and strategic support elsewhere, your coworkers are more likely to support you later down the road. Or at least, less likely to turn on you.

And for those who already have turned against you? Remember that the people who have turned against you since you have found yourself at war with an employer are not the most important people in your life, nor the only people who have ever known or will know you. They are simply one group of people whose views of you are based on misperceptions, rumors and outright lies. No matter what your relationships with them were before, your most valuable relationships are now elsewhere—with many more still to come.

So just where do you find these relationships and develop these new social networks? Through communities, places of worship, clubs, or interest groups. Join a church, volunteer with a political campaign or for a cause that is important to you, take some college classes, check out www.meetup.com for groups that are forming in your area, take up a new hobby, get involved in theater, or get online and join a virtual community. But be careful you don't use these new communities for emotional dumping grounds. Don't vent about what is going on and don't try to bring your new friends and colleagues into your mobbing nightmare. Tell a few, perhaps, as you get to know them, but don't go into detail or discuss it regularly. Let them get to know you a bit before revealing anything about the mobbing or shunning. If you reveal it too soon, they will take it as a red flag that something might be off about you. If they have a chance to get to know you, however, they are more likely to be empathetic.

Some groups, however, may be especially appropriate for turning to for support in the hardest times. Religious communities, therapy groups, groups centered around workplace or mobbing issues, are all appropriate places to come right out and tell what's going on and ask for help. In such places, it is perfectly acceptable to ask for advice, comfort or just understanding. But don't overwhelm them with details. Always be cautious about what you reveal because those who don't understand mobbing or your situation could become cautious of you. You could babble incoherently and constantly and come across as a crazy catastrophe and alienate them before your friendships have even formed. And if your conflict reaches the courts, anyone you've discussed the issue with could be subpoenaed to appear as a witness for or against you. So limit what you share about the mobbing, and allow these new relationships to grow.

The important thing is to create new social communities where you are valued, respected and supported. Seek them out, and if you can't find the one that's right for you, create it. Whatever you do, just ensure that you build support outside the workplace and/or group that is shunning you.

Keep your distance as much as possible, while maintaining your responsibilities to work cooperatively together. If you are fortunate enough to be reading this at an early stage of your mobbing, as soon as any formal investigation commences or any formal declaration is made by someone in management that you are no longer wanted and should start looking for a job, communicate to your closest coworkers that you are going to back off for awhile. Tell them that while things remain up in the air, for their own protection you're going to step back for a bit. Assure them that if you aren't as chatty as usual or don't join the social circles or events, it is because you don't want to put them in a vulnerable position with management. Do not say anything more. Do not tell them you are afraid, that you are angry, or that you are going to see a lawyer. If they ask you about your plans, just say you haven't made any decisions at this point. Assure them, however, that you will always be available for anything they need—you will continue to work with them and cooperate and pitch in and do all you can, just as you always have. Do not say anything self-deprecating (the context and humor will be stripped from the retelling and it will be relayed as a confession of inadequacy), do not say anything negative about your other coworkers or employers, and **do not give in to the temptation to vent**. Just sigh and tell them that it looks like the wolves are at the door and it's best to lay low until it's over. Nothing more than that.

If the mobbing has progressed, however, it may be too late for that. Your coworkers may well have already started to shun and devour you. If you haven't yet left your job and are continuing to work with the employer who is attempting to push you out, you are having to continuously interact with the very people who want to damage your standing and reputation, defend their aggression against you, and have been told or have told the most unimaginably hurtful and untrue things about you. And they have seen you at your very worse—obsessing over the wrongs done to you, and maybe even crying, screaming, or raging at the injustice you have suffered. They may well be looking at you as if you are crazy when you do so much as make a photocopy or get a drink of water. Just walking down the hall can be torture when all eyes are on—or turn away from—you and any moment can bring a new trick or attack.

Always maintain professional and collegial interactions. Do not be snippy, sulky or refuse to talk to someone you must communicate with to do your job. Continue to ask them for information when you need to, solicit their input, include them in decision making, and share information that is relevant to them—even if you know they are jackals who want to pounce the minute they can and take credit for all your hard work. Do as much on email as possible (keeping it to the minimum, but in a friendly tone) so that you have a cyber-trail of cooperation, but when necessary, interact in person. Exude confidence and normalcy, even if inside you feel like your head is about to burst into flames and your heart is beating so hard you fear it will fly right out of you. Fake it. (That's a good time to role play.)

If you are able to work remotely from home, by all means do so, as much as possible. But be careful that you don't risk being accused of not being available. Communicate regularly electronically, and make regular on-site appearances. Do not miss meetings or other group activities where you are expected to appear. By working remotely, however, you do risk being further isolated, made the subject of gossip, and overlooked for professional opportunities—you are out of sight, and that makes it easier to attack you, and easier to ignore you. But if you are going to be attacked and ignored anyway, then for your own emotional survival it may be best to work off-site. (But do not do so without discussing it first with your attorney, if you have one, and getting written consent from your employers that you have their permission to do so.)

More likely, you cannot work remotely from home or if you do, you risk being accused of not meeting your professional responsibilities. In these cases, work in your office, and keep the door partially or fully closed. If you work in an open space or cubicle, do your best to tune the others out. Visualize yourself working in a circus tent if need be, and everyone around you is just another clown.

Do not join in group social activities, and do not expect to be invited or wanted at them. No matter how popular or inside the golden circle you once were, things have changed. You are now a target, and that means you need to keep your distance. Let them get together for happy hour, mill around the coffeemaker, go out for power lunches or a round of golf. You have work to do (and new networks to foster). Smile, be cheerful, and decline any invitations with an apology that you'd love to join them, but you have a deadline to meet or a meeting to attend. Don't be specific. Keep them guessing.

An exception: birthdays, baby showers, retirements and any other event honoring someone you work with or for. If they are off-site, send a gift and card but be politely unavailable. On-site, sing Happy Birthday, smile and applaud, then slip away discretely and get back to work. Failure to appear at these events will be noted in the gossip, and rapidly escalate to some godawful social affront you supposedly committed. Don't give them that bone to gnaw on. Show up, smile, extend your good wishes, and retreat. Nothing more and nothing less.

Develop compassion for your coworkers. Here's another tough one, perhaps toughest of all, and the one I receive the most flack over for suggesting. But it's one of the most important if you want to survive and recover. To survive the mob, you have to simultaneously avoid them and interact with them. As you do so, you are hurting tremendously, and you have learned not to trust them, but to fear them. You have also come to hate them. But what you need to do is humanize them—if for no better reason than it helps to diffuse their power to hurt you.

As noted in the previous chapter, one technique you can try to soften the pain of encountering them is to imagine your coworkers as silly or benign. But more importantly, you have to learn to have compassion for them even if, perhaps *especially* if, they have abused you, violated you, damaged your career and reputation, or cost you your job, and then some. By learning to have compassion, you begin to understand mobbing as something all humans do when acting in groups, and you begin to feel—even if they cannot—the underlying fear and confusion that is motivating their aggression—and in turn it becomes less about you, and more about the atmosphere the mobbing has created.

Having compassion does not mean forgiving. You do not have to forgive those who have seriously harmed you. But the more you work on seeing them as flawed humans, the more that you can see their aggression as a weakness, and the less rage you will feel. And the less rage you feel, the faster you will heal—and the less threatening you will appear to others.

Feeling compassion for someone who has done you so much harm does not come easy. It will take time, and it may never come at all. But no matter how vicious they may be—and many will be vicious—when they are mobbing you they are acting like terrified and troubled humans—just as you, too, are terrified and troubled as you endure their abuse. And as hard as it may be to accept, just as in warfare, **each side views itself as acting in self defense, not in offense**. Understanding this discomforting reality helps to see that even the most aggressive person believes their acts are somehow justified and that they are protecting themselves, however weirdly.

Remember, when humans believe someone deserves abusive treatment, there is no limit to how abusive they will become. It is for this reason that when you read many comments, articles or books by people opposed to bullying, they will advocate the same, if not worse, aggressive treatment toward the person they identify as a bully. They will argue that bullies deserve to be expelled from the workplace and never hired again. They will argue that bullies deserve to be deprived of their civil rights, or beaten up or publicly shamed. By convincing themselves that someone is deserving of bad treatment, even the kindest people persuade themselves that their behavior is not aggressive—it's justice. And what that means is that the people who are mobbing you have convinced themselves that what they're doing to you is not aggressive, it is not mobbing, it is not bullying, and it is not bad. They have convinced themselves that it is righteous and necessary and their actions are noble.

When we are at war—either as nations or as humans engaging in a legal battle—we see the other side as different from ourselves. But compassion is not about seeing the differences between ourselves and those who have harmed us. It's about recognizing the common features that make us human. After all, if you are honest with yourself, you will see that no matter how justified your complaint against your employer and how abusive they have been toward you, that you, too, have been exhibiting some of your worse qualities since you crossed them.

You may have exposed your vulnerabilities, reacted swiftly and force-fully, sobbed or swore to high heavens. However you reacted, it has been a human response. They are responding like humans, as well. You don't by any means need to excuse them or forgive them. But recognizing their humanity, however badly it's displayed, will help *you* to recover. And it will help insure that you do not become mobbed in the next job—because you will have a more compassionate view of your new coworkers, a compassion tempered with wisdom and a better understanding of how human nature is expressed in an organizational setting.

Remain cheerful but private. Do not share personal information and do not gossip. Meanwhile, back at the office, how do you handle your coworkers? You're keeping your distance as best as you can, you're being polite and cooperative. But people will be pestering you, even while they're shunning you. Some will be trying to get you to crack, or get some dirt on you, or maybe some genuinely care. But as people distance themselves from you, you'll get those calls and visits from "concerned" coworkers, most of whom aren't really concerned. So what are you going to do, hang up on them?

The truth is, as the shunning begins you very much want to talk to your coworkers. You want them to like you, to include you in their conversations and continue to interact with you just as they always did before the mobbing and shunning began. So how do you keep your distance and not get further shunned?

Some people are very private by nature, while others are an open book. Most fall in between. But whichever you are, it's time to become more private. Remain as cheerful as you can, but keep your private life to yourself. When you do talk with someone at work or elsewhere, be careful that you don't ramble or babble. Rambling and babbling are common side effects of mobbing, but they are also high-risk behaviors. Learn to catch yourself at the first sign of a ramble or a babble. It will only provoke your emotional flooding, intensify your pain, make you look crazy and drive your friends away.

Be careful, as well, about the information you do share. Don't talk about your children, don't share your views about the latest scandal. Don't talk about dating, your marriage, your divorce or your hobbies or even the latest movie that you saw if it contains sex or violence or is on any topic that is remotely provocative or controversial (which pretty much eliminates them all).

It's amazing how easily completely innocent trivia can be turned into a rumor or sliced and diced until it fits precisely into the new image that's being crafted of you. You mention your teenagers are taxing you these days: "She's always complaining, even about her own children." You share in a conversation about a problematic client: "He's really starting to show his dark side, now he's even criticizing his own clients." You jest about your internet dating adventures: "Of course she can't maintain a working relationship, she can't even keep a boyfriend." You mention going out to dinner or on a weekend vacation: "He's hardly suffering, from the way he talks he's been having the time of his life." You join in the water-cooler conversation about the TV show that aired the night before: "She is fixated on violent movies; you should have seen her eyes when she was talking about that serial killer, Dexter."

So when the "concerned" calls come in, just thank them for thinking of you and tell them that work is the last thing you want to talk about. Rapidly shift the conversation to *them*—how are they doing? By listening to others, you get out of your own head and strengthen your empathy and compassion, while at the same time you protect yourself from further attacks that might come from letting something perfectly innocent slip past your lips and into the ears of a conniving gossiper.

Remember—it's not so much what *you* say, as what the *listener* will say once they start trashing you in the gossip circles. So not only do you want to be discreet in public conversations—where people can reinforce each other's interpretation easily once they start to gossip—but **be very careful about the coworker who comes to you with "concern," asking how you are holding up and prying for information**. No matter how sincere they might be, do not give them any information. Smile, thank them for their concern, and assure them you are doing your best and keeping your focus on your work. Nothing more, nothing less. Then document the encounter. (At the same time, don't be the least bit rude; if they are genuinely reaching out to you, the last thing you should do is rebuff them; be polite, but not informative.)

If you find that's difficult, however, and you slip back into talking about work or yourself a little too easily, just catch yourself and if you're on the phone, say there's a knock at the door, there's something boiling over in the kitchen or your neighbor's stuffing a naked corpse in the trunk of their car and you need to film it for YouTube. If you're talking in person, tell them you need to get back to work, or you're running late for an appointment. But get off the phone, or exit the conversation wherever it is and superglue your mouth shut.

But what if they aren't talking about you? What if you find yourself in a gossip circle at work and they're chatting about someone or something else? Again, be extra careful, and under no circumstances, agree with anything disparaging about anyone.

It might seem obvious by now, but the truth is, gossip confers belonging to a group. To be excluded from the office gossip is a hallmark of shunning—and to be included marks you as a trusted coworker. So you may find yourself tempted to participate in gossip or even to pass some on yourself. Resist the temptation, no matter how salacious or damaging to your adversary's reputation, no matter how much you might want to be included in the group. **Gossip is what is going to kill your reputation while your complaint against your employer (or their complaint against you) progresses**. Do not participate. And if you do, no matter how much others may have been agreeing with you at the time, be assured that you will find yourself accused of spreading lies. Their gossip will be treated as gospel. Yours will be treated as something else entirely. Stay away.

And though it should go without saying, avoid any situation with coworkers that involves alcohol. Do not drink in the presence of your coworkers (or use drugs, obviously, not even if you're all a bunch of pot heads). If you work in the wine business, start spitting. No matter how many people are drinking, you do not want to drink. At the same time, you do not want people to suggest you're not drinking because you "have a problem" which they very well might do if mobbing has commenced. If questions about why you aren't drinking start, just say you aren't feeling like it, you're driving, you're dieting, or you're having a colonoscopy in the morning, or whatever you can say to shut them up.

Focus on your support system, not your haters. When the people you work with day in and day out send you the message that they want you gone, it isn't long before you begin to internalize those messages, feeling increasingly horrible and inadequate as you walk down the halls, sit at the meetings, and try to get your work done. It soon begins to feel as if *everyone* wants you gone, and in time, most everyone you work with will want you gone once you are involved in a battle with your employer.

And while it might seem obvious and trite, the truth is, you have to begin to focus on the support that you do have. Yet these support systems are also vulnerable to damage because in every sphere of your life, you will be hyper-sensitive to criticism, easily wounded, and an incredible drag to be around.

To counter that normal reaction to mobbing, start a journal listing all the people in your life who support you, like you, and love you. Do not include anyone from your workplace, because those people will increasingly turn away and when they do, crossing them off your list will make you feel increasingly abandoned. The objective is to add to this list, and you do that by expanding your social networks outside your work and profession, and by focusing more on how you can be a good friend and neighbor to those around you.

In your journal, note what it is that you like about the person who supports you, and what they like about you. What gives you the confidence that they care about you? Do they tell you clearly that they like you and why? Do they show their care and support? Do they listen to you? Do they call or visit? Do they keep in touch through letters, email or text messages? Have they written letters of recommendation for you, done you a favor, given you a gift? Have they invited you into their home, introduced you to their friends, family or colleagues? Have they put up with you at your worst, and been kind but honest when you have needed their counsel?

Now reverse these questions to ask yourself if you've done these things for them. If not, you know two things—that people may care very much about you without your having done much to show or express it in return. And you also know that you have a lot to catch up on when it comes to letting the people who care about you know how much you care about them—and not from a drunken confession, but from sincerely reaching out to do something for the people in your life who count.

Always remember that no matter how loud, vocal and large the mob condemning you may be, these are the people who count. These are the people to whom you owe your gratitude and support for their own needs, and these are the people whose views of you matter. Do not exhaust them with your emotional flooding, do not expect them to be there constantly, on-call, ready to drop everything to help you, and do not expect them to take risks for you at this point, such as signing anything supporting you. It is not because they won't—some will and most won't take risks for you or anyone else—and it does not mean that they are not sincere friends or supporters if they don't. But because you are in an emotionally vulnerable state right now, you do not want to set yourself up for rejection by testing the support of those around you. Simply focus on the caring, love, support and friendship that is offered you each day, in whatever form it comes, and it will come to you.

Volunteer. I've already suggested volunteering, but I want to empha-size it because it makes a huge difference. When your world is crumbling beneath you, it's time to step into someone else's world. One of the most effective ways you can build other social networks and friendships is to volunteer to help others. You'll have to set your pain aside, which is not easy to do, and be careful not to talk about your work or the problems you're having there, but if you have the emotional ability, get out and help someone else. Volunteer with Ronald McDonald House to help families whose children are dying. Volunteer at the zoo or an animal shelter to help animals if you're an animal person. Volunteer to teach a child or an adult how to read. Volunteer to cook for someone who is elderly, ill or disabled or just plain alone.

The important thing is to recognize that as painful and overwhelming as the mobbing may be, there are people who are suffering far greater and far more insurmountable pains with amazing grace and courage. There are others out there even weaker than you whose lives are subject to the cruelties of this world and they need help. And you have skills and abilities that you can share with others to help them to grow and develop. And if you do volunteer to help others, you just might forge a new career should the one you're in collapse.

Enduring the mob is a hellish task, and whatever your weaknesses, foibles, past errors or missteps, you do not deserve such treatment. But the uncomfortable truth is, life is filled with undeserved tests and trials, and it is up to you to conquer this one. You can, and you will, if you do not give in to the escalating rage and self-loathing that being mobbed inevitably provokes.

Keep in mind that those who are mobbing you are not responding to you, as much as they are responding to gossip, fear, and organizational leadership. But that knowledge hardly helps you. Being shunned and treated badly by the people in our lives hurts like hell.

To a great extent, you must endure it. But now you know that there are some things you can do to keep from providing them additional fodder and ammunition to facilitate their attacks. By keeping your emotions and reactions in check, retreating, and staying as productive and focused on others as possible, you will slowly rebuild your reputation and minimize their power over your spirit. In the meantime, you also have to do everything you possibly can to protect your career, because workplace mobbing means someone's out to damage it.

CHAPTER 8

Protect Yourself Professionally

Here's the deal: mobbing can kill your career. It can kill it through rumors and gossip and intentional lies. It can kill it by cutting you off from the social networks that make it possible to enjoy professional opportunities, to get a job and to be recognized in your field. And it can kill your career by being so psychologically wounding and traumatizing that you can no longer work and your brain may actually be changed, your emotional strength nearly crippled, and your sense of hope for the future so darkened all you see before you is the black, blood darkness of a dawn that never comes. In other words, once mobbing commences, you have to scramble to safeguard your career just when your capacity to do so is at its lowest.

And it's this mortal blow to one's career that has so many of your co-workers and friends turning against you—they know what's up ahead for them if they support you, and you're missing the lifeboat if you don't get it, too. So get it—these are dastardly times and you've got the choice to sink or swim. Here's how to swim.

Assume you are constantly monitored. Just because they're out to get you doesn't mean you're paranoid. But as an FBI agent once told me, if they are out to get you, it pays to be paranoid. Always assume that there are cameras watching you. If I had said this a decade ago you would have had cause to consider me nuts. But these days, there are cameras everywhere; in the hallways, in the bathrooms and even in your office or cubicle. Do not do anything stupid like defacing the public space, or even your own office.

Assume every keystroke you log on your computer is being monitored and recorded. Almost always, once a mobbing starts, management alerts the technology folks to keep an eye on what you're up to. That means **do not go shopping on the internet, do not check out dating sights, do not log on to Facebook or Twitter and do not use your workplace computer for any personal use**. I can't state this warning clearly enough, and it is probably the most disregarded—and important—piece of advice I can give to any mobbing target. You shouldn't be doing any of this stuff anyway, but most workers do, and if you can't stop, then they have cause to fire your ass. Get it together and segregate your personal life from your professional life.

That also means do not send any personal emails, or especially emails seeking advice or discussing your problems at work, from an email account your employer has assigned you, even if you do so from your own computer. I regularly receive emails from mobbing targets who are writing me for advice from their work email accounts. Never do that!

Every worker should follow this advice at all times, whether mobbed or not. An even better piece of advice is to get your own laptop which is used only for work and not connected to your workplace servers. Unfortunately, in many if not most cases, that is not practical advice. Either the workplace servers are necessary for you to access, and/or you cannot afford a separate computer just for workplace use.

At the same time, you should never use your personal computer for workplace use, because once you do, you risk having to turn over the hard drive in the event your conflict gets to the courts. If you have used your personal computer for workplace use, and if you sue your employer (or someone from work sues you), you can be compelled to turn over that hard drive. So in other words, use the workplace computer only for work use, and/or get a separate computer just for work. Do not use your personal computer(s) for workplace use and vice-versa. (And that includes smart phones and iPads.)

Here's a story. I was a well-respected academic when I was mobbed and I reacted forcefully and swiftly. I raged and sent out raging emails telling the whole world what was going on. I was convinced that the only way my employers could get away with their crap was by operating in secrecy. I thought that if I told people what they were doing that people would rally to support me. I was wrong.

I soon found myself marginalized, then ostracized, and before long, there wasn't anything short of bestiality that I wasn't being accused of. It wasn't long after I was accused of nuclear terrorism (really) that a student dropped by my office and after some innocuous conversation, asked how things were going.

I hadn't made a secret of what was going on, as you know by now. At the same time, my public outrage aside, I otherwise prided myself on maintaining boundaries with my students. So I said something to the effect that it sucked but I was focused on my teaching. And that's when he began talking about details of my case that I hadn't disclosed to anyone.

I didn't really know this student. We had vastly different political positions, but I respected his contributions to class. He was an older student, and not naïve by any means. But he wasn't even a student in my department, and his knowledge of the details of my case disturbed me. I wasn't sure if he had access to information about my case or if he was just super-insightful. But his conversation suggested that he knew something I didn't know. And that was disconcerting.

I didn't know if he had been sent as "a spy" to keep an eye on me, or if he was trying to be helpful. I didn't know if he was nuts or brilliant. But his casual conversation became increasingly creepy until he finally said something startling.

"Just be careful about your computer."

"Oh, yeah, I know," I flippantly replied. "I don't use it for anything personal anymore, but God knows what they'll pull off of it."

"Oh, you don't have to worry about what they'll pull off of it."

"Of course I do," I said. "I never worried about it before so I would order things off Amazon, send personal emails, Google whatever entertained me." I thought of all the times I pondered how to decorate the playroom, what beauty cream I should buy to keep from aging or what toy I should buy for my daughter. I even mail ordered bras off my computer, and shuddered to think what they'd make of my inadequate bra size.

"No, you don't have to worry about what they'll take *off* it," he said in a somber, ominous voice, "You need to worry about what they'll put *on* it."

And that's when he told me he worked in the law school and had handled many employee appeals, and had come across a case where, he alleged, my employer was supposedly trying to be rid of a tenured employee and had systematically, over several months, loaded child porn onto his computer.

"The only problem was," he said, "they had the wrong sex. They didn't know he was gay, so they got caught."

Now I have no way of knowing whether what he said was true or not, but when he followed by advising me to unplug the computer and never turn it on again, that's exactly what I did. Until that time I had, in my paranoid thinking, put a Post-It Note over the computer camera, something that years later I still think was a sensible thing to do. But it wasn't until I was told that for all they might take off my computer, they had the ability to put anything they wanted onto it, that I realized just how far my employers might go.

Now understand. My employers went far. They demonstrated that there was absolutely nothing they wouldn't say about me, nothing they wouldn't do, to destroy me. They even reported my then-ten year old daughter to the FBI Joint Terrorism Task Force after hearing she had suggested I bake cookies for the head of my department. Because he was a diabetic, they considered it a threat.

I soon learned that my former friends and colleagues would soon do the same. But nothing at all about what I experienced was unique to me.

What happened to me was predictable and routine—I just hadn't predicted it or considered it routine.

Most people won't have the FBI Joint Terrorism Task Force knocking on their door because they're being mobbed. In my case, it was possible because I was studying nuclear material, specifically, the health and environmental effects of depleted uranium, which my employers were paying me to study. But that's all they needed to paint me as overly fascinated by the subject, and it wasn't long before they claimed that I was engaged in extortion to obtain classified information and was planning to build an H-Bomb.

Anyone working with money can be accused of trying to steal it—even if no money was ever stolen. Anyone working with children can be accused of pedophilia. Anyone working in the military can be accused of violence. The nature of your work can and will be used against you if at all possible, once they're determined to be rid of you.

All employers at all times will do whatever they can to destroy the profession of someone they become convinced is a "difficult employee." They will lie. They will spy. And they will vilify. So do not, under any circumstances, make it easy for them to do so.

In addition to not using your computer for personal use or your personal computer for workplace use, do not use your workplace phone for personal use and always assume that your workplace phone is monitored and the calls are recorded. If your employer owns your cell phone, assume it's monitored.

Always assume there's a nanny-cam pointed at you when you're at work, and always assume you're just being cautious and that you're really not being watched. You need to balance protecting yourself with not being paranoid, so the best bet is to never do or say anything at work you don't want to see uploaded onto YouTube.

Get the resume out. Always make your resume portable. That means that even if you aren't looking for a job, it doesn't hurt to have people considering you for a job. And if you are being mobbed, all the more reason to be out there interviewing. Update your resume, contact head-hunters, peruse employment options, apply for jobs—but multiply your options.

Stay off Facebook and other social media other than what you need to do to maintain a professional profile. And for God's sake, do not say anything about your work, your employer, your coworkers or any of that on the internet. Do not even leave an anonymous comment on a blog or forum, unless it is written on a personal computer in which you do not do anything work-related, and does not reveal any information about your workplace or smear your employer. Here's why.

Obviously, if you criticize them openly on a public forum you can be fired, or at the very least find yourself explaining your comments to various administrators and/or investigators, which isn't going to help you at all. You may think they've never seen it, only to find they've turned it over to the EEOC or your attorneys, long down the road. Or your comments may be seen by a potential employer thinking of hiring you. And even if you weren't criticizing your employer or bitching about your work, using any work time or computers for posting to Facebook, no matter how common, is unprofessional and if someone is out to get you, will be added to the heap of accusations against you. Do not do it.

As for anonymous comments, if you file a lawsuit, you will be asked about such things, under oath, first in a deposition and later at a trial (if it gets that far). If you lie and you're caught, it's perjury. If the comment was written on a workplace computer, they'll find it. If it was written on your own, but you also did work for your employer on that computer, it's possible they will succeed in compelling you to turn over your hard drive. Just don't do it.

If you have an Amazon Wish List, delete it, unless it's completely benign. Those lists are public, and act like bridal registries for the internet. They are traceable by your email address. Protect your privacy and don't use it.

And now, go to all your Twitter, Facebook, Linked-In and other social media sites and start deleting all the stupid things you've put up there. Get anything off that criticizes your employer, complains about work, or mentions problems at work. (If you have already filed a lawsuit and been told not to destroy evidence, consult with your attorney about whether or not you can delete such entries. Chances are you can't.)

Clean up anything that shows you half-dressed, undressed, your tongue hanging out, holding or talking about drinking or drugs, or anything else that a potential employer is likely to look at and then cross you off their list.

Now stay off those sites. Don't keep putting immature and unprofessional and dumb stuff up online.

Don't focus on what others are doing at work; focus on your own work. It's easy to start wondering who is being assigned to what project, what is working with what client, who has gotten what raise or perk. If you are being mobbed, you have good reason to want to know what your co-workers and managers are up to. And you have good reason to want them to show concern for what is happening to you that's making it so hard to focus on your work. But the smartest thing you can do right now if you are being mobbed is to focus on your own work.

Don't think about what other people are up to or what perks they might be getting for helping to destroy you. It will destroy you to think about it. This is a time when anything you have worked on can be credited to someone else, when anyone who attacks you can be praised and promoted, and when all the resources previously channeled to you—your salary, your benefits, your clients, your office—can be reallocated to someone else. The jackals will be lining up, and justifying the spoils of their pillage by making you out to be the bad guy.

If you spend your time thinking about how wrong it is for others to benefit from your pain and productivity, then you will suffer all the more. Other people are going to exploit you and take advantage of your losses. Other people are not only going to take credit for your hard work, but they are going to be comforted for having had to put up with you in the process. Anything you say or do to take credit for your own work will only work against you.

Getting angry at them is only going to work against you—if it's displayed, you're a danger; if it's internalized, your mind, body and soul will be in danger.

Accept that you're getting screwed and skewered and focus on working even harder. Use the techniques discussed in Chapter Six to kick those thoughts of the mobbers right out of your head. Focus on your own work, not on theirs. And once they do appropriate your work as their own, it's theirs, even if you did it. So do your very best to keep focusing on what you *need to do* to get ahead in your profession, not on what you *have* done or on what *has been done* to you.

Do everything you can to work as hard as you can and to make a name for yourself. But don't tell your coworkers what you're doing. Inform them only to the extent you must to keep yourself employed and counter the attacks against you, but downplay your achievements—and keep them focused on what you can do to land a job outside your current place of employment, not on bettering the workplace. You could discover a cure for cancer and no one would applaud you if you are being mobbed, at least no one in the workplace. Just focus on getting the job done and trust that outside the workplace what you're doing will matter.

More importantly, do your best at all times to concentrate on meeting your own obligations, and not on expecting others to respect or help you. This is the time to set your ego aside—when it is being most attacked. Just produce and produce and produce. To the extent that you're too beat up to do so, don't beat yourself up any further. Just do your best, but try hard to do even better.

Bite your tongue and conform. Do not express any contrarian positions and consistently go along with the majority in decision making, voting, and discussions. This can be a hard one, but you've got to do it. No matter how idiotic an idea that a coworker or boss presents, no matter how much it outrages you, *keep your views to yourself.* Resist the urge to offer a better idea, point out the flaws in an argument, or remind the boss that the great idea your coworker was just praised for, was your idea in the first place. Follow the crowd, agree with the majority, and hold your tongue in meetings and other discussions, except to express agreement. That's what most of them are doing anyway—learn from them, at least for the time being. You can be creative and assertive elsewhere, but not here, not now.

Do not discuss your problems with your employer with anyone at work. I've said this before and I'll say it again—don't go there. Don't bring up the topic, don't take the bait if others bring it up. Don't disparage your employer, and don't seek out support. Let it go, because no one in the workplace can be counted on to help you, no matter how much they may want to do so and no matter how much they dislike or are being abused by your employer. Focus on your work, not your workplace.

Do not react to their attacks. You already know what's going to happen. People are going to call you all kinds of things. They'll say that you're a liar, that you're always complaining, that you make all sorts of accusations, that you're never satisfied. They'll say that you've got mental problems, that you're crazy, that you're delusional. They'll say that you've always been a problem, that you're attacking everyone, that you're a bully and widely disliked. If you're white, they might say you're a racist. If you're black, they might say that you think everyone is a racist. If you're a man you might be accused of sexual harassment, if you're a woman you might be accused of being a slut. Nothing about your actual beliefs, practices, or work record will make a damned bit of difference. The truth is that they're going to make shit up and people will believe it—even your close friends.

And you're going to have to just put up with it. Absurd as that sounds— and I would have been among the most appalled by such a statement, back before I was mobbed—if you want to survive with your reputation intact, you have to keep your mouth shut *and let other people defend you.*

Unfortunately, you might die of old age before your coworkers come to your defense, but if you try to defend yourself and no one speaks up—and few if anyone will—then you're just howling in the wind. Let them call you a pedophilic terrorist who wears white after Labor Day, but *do not react.*

Get support for your position elsewhere—outside your professional circles. You should go to great lengths to keep your workplace conflicts confined to the workplace, no matter how abusive your employers have been. For many targets of workplace mobbing and bullying, this advice flies in the face of concerns for social justice—when someone violates our rights and security, we tend to want them exposed and punished. But no matter how flagrant their abuse, if at all possible keep it confined to the workplace walls so that future employers do not learn of it, at least until there is a serious discussion about hiring you.

Ironically, like telling a big lie, the greater the abuse against you, the more likely others will assign blame to you. That is because people tend to think that an employer would not go to such lengths to hurt an employee unless they really had it coming. Of course, there's no truth to such a belief at all; all it takes is for one or two cruel people in a position of leadership to get the ball rolling, and the cruelty will grow exponentially. It will snowball into an avalanche of cruelty the harder you fight back and the longer you stay. It has nothing to do with wrongdoing on your part, and in fact, the greater your own wrongdoing, the less likely they will mob you. That is because if you really are violating workplace rules, laws or ethics, or you really are disruptive to the workplace or abusing other employees, it's not that hard to get rid of you. It may be necessary to make a case, but it won't require the escalating cascade of accusations necessary to be rid of a valuable employee.

And what that means is that if you really are having your rights violated at work, keeping it within the walls of the workplace as much as possible will safeguard you from libelous smears (libel is much harder to prosecute in court than you might realize, and likely to boomerang and bring more attention to the lies, rather than discredit them). It will also protect you from the misperceptions of outsiders who will hesitate to work with you because they will assume that "there are two sides to every story" (which is not true—there are as many sides to every story as there are characters in it, and yours is just one of them). And it will protect you from outsiders judging you to be a troublemaker who just can't cut it.

Nonetheless, sometimes you do have to take steps to garner support, particularly if you have been terminated unjustly for a crime or ethical violation, or had your professional reputation smeared beyond the workplace. In that case, be cautious. By appealing to your professional organizations, you may find that they respond by contacting your employer only to come away convinced that you're the problem. Then you will have done serious damage to your professional reputation. In other cases, appealing to outside organizations could bring your conflict to the pages of local, national, or professional publications, and before you know it, you're branded not just as a troublemaker, but an unwanted and disliked employee and loser, even if you're presented in a sympathetic light. People don't want to align with falling stars; they want to align with rising ones. They don't want to hire damaged goods; they want to hire durable goods.

So seek your support through groups that are not affiliated with your profession, but are instead there to help you understand your rights and offer professional guidance. Anti-bully advocacy groups may be useful, but they can also pose a danger if they adopt inflexible explanatory models for workplace bullying which fail to distinguish between interpersonal bullying and group mobbing; distinguish people as "good" or "bad" while demonizing the "bad" and painting the "good" as faultless, and encourage lawsuits and ongoing battles with the employer.

Workplace support groups that assist whistleblowers, such as PEER (Public Employees for Environmental Responsibility) which focuses on helping government workers who have blown the whistle on environmental violations or cover-ups, may be a good source of support. Groups that help workers to strategize effective re-employment plans, or otherwise help people to safeguard their emotional wellbeing and legal rights in the face of job loss may be useful.

Certain civil rights groups may also be helpful. For example, the ACLU may be effective in advocating for your position, without bringing the conflict into public view. FIRE, the Foundation for Individual Rights in Education, a First Amendments rights group, can be quite helpful if you are accused of violating politically correct speech codes in the university, or facing unjust accusations of sexual harassment, but I've found them completely disinterested in assisting people who have been subjected to sexual harassment or discrimination and had their First Amendment rights breached as a result.

Finally, be extremely cautious about going to the press, no matter how egregious the violations against you, and no matter how sympathetic the reporter. Most reporters can't report a kitchen fire accurately these days; reporters are no longer taught to interview subjects, investigate stories, ask follow-up questions or distinguish between evidence and accusation. They're trained to get page view clicks by sensationalizing the story. They may very well screw it up, and then you're facing even more problems. They may quote you saying something stupid that your employer can use against you—maybe something that could lead to a libel suit against you. Or they may actually do their job and investigate, contacting former employers and associates, and before you know it, your entire profession has heard about it and assuming you've done something wrong, leading your colleagues outside your workplace to start recalling you in a whole new—and adverse—light.

But supposing the reporter really wants to help you, and really wants to tell your story. You might think that is just fine and dandy if they present you in a golden light. But once they do, others will come along to respond to the story, presenting "new information" that may or may not be true, but will effectively discredit the story presenting your side.

Another possible if not probable result from going to the press is that when your employer is contacted, they are likely to say "no comment," while suggesting you have had problems for some time, that you have caused problems for other employees, and that you are mentally ill and/or lying. They may well even call you a bully—which in this day and age, may be all that a reporter needs to hear before closing the book on you. "Oh, he's a bully; I didn't realize. Well, thank you, I'll pass that information on to my editor and I doubt we'll be contacting you again. Thank you for your time." Story killed.

Another high risk of going to reporters is that they'll present your side, then "the other side," and readers will assume that regardless of the complaints against your employer, you "did something to bring it on." People don't like to think that they could face a sudden attack on their career for no reason. It is much easier to assume it only happens to people who do something to bring it on.

If the press is approached, it is far better that someone else approach them on your behalf. Defending yourself tends to work against you; if others will appeal to the press on your behalf, and you are respectful but offer no comment, you are more likely to be well perceived than if you are your own PR person.

Finally, if you do go to the press, it's out there. Permanently. You may well put this matter behind you, but five, ten, fifteen years on down the road, if someone wants to cause you trouble again, it's only a Google away to discover they only need to repeat what was said by your former employer. Rarely does going to the press help a worker, even if the coverage is on their side.

Make the press your last resort; check out the publication and the reporter; tape-record all conversations for yourself; make sure they have a well-organized (and not overwhelming) record of your achievements and strong evaluations demonstrating you were formerly well-respected, and present your case in a non-emotional manner without smearing your employer. Stick to the facts and let the facts show, don't tell, your story.

Secure communications, computers, email accounts. Just as I've indicated you shouldn't be using your personal computers for work, or your work computers (or phones) for personal use, and segregating your email accounts, you must also secure them. Be sure all your computers are password protected, and that the password is not easily guessable, and contains numbers, symbols and letters. Do not use the same passwords on your work and personal computers. Ditto for smart phones. And when you walk away from your computer, even for a few moments, put it into a password-protected sleep mode. Even if your employer is behaving and not monitoring you (although they have the right to monitor equipment they own and space they control), you do not want to wander away from your computer to use the bathroom, only to have the opportunist in the next office stroll by and peer at your computer to see what you've been up to—or to log onto that porn or drug site so that you'll be blamed.

Mobbing is permission to be aggressive, and when humans have that permission, they go for it. They will hurt you just for fun. They will hurt you just to score points with the boss. And then they'll justify it by convincing themselves it's your own fault. Secure your workspace and computers and cell phones and email accounts at home and at work. Cover up that camera on your monitor, if not with a Post-It Note, then with some sort of decoration that doesn't look so obvious. Keep your cell phone with you at all times, and never use it for personal use at work, unless it's for very quick and important messages.

Keep your office door locked if you have a locking office door. Same with your desk. Consider installing a nanny-cam yourself, to see if anyone's coming in. Take photos of your desktop and interior of an unlocked top-desk drawer every night and compare it in the morning (though any changes in the desktop could be the cleaning person, but depending on how things have been rearranged, you may well be able to recognize if it was an office snoop).

Finally, download some file-shredding software to get rid of anything you've already stupidly downloaded onto your computer and need to clean up—unless you have been instructed not to destroy evidence (in which case, consult your attorney). Also download the best spyware you can find. It takes little effort for someone to download a keystroke logger onto your computer (don't try doing that to theirs; you may very well get caught if they are monitoring the office with cameras). Key Scrambler, Spy Bot Search and Destroy, RoboForm2Go, and the top firewall programs are all well reviewed.

Get email tracking software. If you want to know if they're even reading your emails (the more you rant and ramble, the more likely they just ignore them and automatically forward them to the legal department), or if you want to know if your coworkers are betraying you, a useful tool is to download some email tracking software. These programs allow you to type in a suffix at the end of an email address, and when the recipient receives the email, they will not see the suffix and never know you're tracking the destiny of your emails (unless of course you're using your work computer and your employers are monitoring it).

You will be notified when they open the email; how long it was opened for (did they even read it?), who they forwarded it to, and if they deleted it. So, for example, if you are being mobbed and things have really heated up, you could send a friendly email to a coworker saying something like, "I misplaced my file on the Smith case; did I leave it in your office?"

In a normal working environment, your coworker would respond, "No, sorry, it's not here, but I'll let you know if I find it." But in a mobbing situation that has reached a high level, the coworker would likely have been instructed to forward any emails you send them. In that case, you might very well receive the friendly reply—along with a notification indicating that shortly after receiving the email, the coworker forwarded it to your manager. That would be useful information.

Then, to mitigate any damage from the accusation that you are disorganized and lost an important file, wait a few hours (or right after receiving your notification that they forwarded the email), then send a follow-up, saying, "Found it! It was here all along, but buried under a pile. Thanks for checking."

Another useful benefit to this software is that as you email various administrative levels, such as if you are involved in an internal investigation or an appeal or anything that requires communicating with differing administrative offices, you can quickly see who is in the loop, and who is answering to whom. You won't see the content of their communications, but you will at least quickly discern the communication channels.

To be most effective, use an email account that is unaffiliated with your workplace, such as a Gmail or Yahoo account, but which you only use for work-related communications, and be sure your emails are sent and received on a computer the workplace does not own and you only use for work. Doing so will minimize the chance that they will discover your own spying.

Of course, that is probably not practical throughout your workday, so a good strategy is to send the important communications from home, as if you are working at home because you are sick, or working from home because it's after hours. (It's also a good rule of thumb to use your work hours only for work, and address your conflicts with your employer after hours as much as possible, to prevent them from making the claim that "your" problems are taking up your work time.)

By regularly sending your emails from a personal account (one only used for work-related communications), your coworkers will become accustomed to it and won't be suspicious of receiving emails from you from a personal email account once you've started using the tracking software.

Some of the highest rated email tracking software include Read Notify (www.readnotify.com), Did They Read It (www.didtheyreadit.com), and Email Secure (www.e-mailsecure.com).

Google yourself regularly. Your employer is going to Google you. Your prospective employer is going to Google you. Anyone investigating you or a complaint you've filed, is probably going to Google you. So you'd be wise to Google you. See what is out there about you—or about other people with your name. Google your name with and without quotes. Google your full name, and Google any derivatives of your name. Google "in blog: "Your Name" to see if there are any comments you have left (or have been left about you). Google your email address, your physical address and your phone number. Google "images" to see if there are any unwanted pictures out there. Switch to Bing, Google Chrome, Firefox and other search engines, to see what there is about you.

If what you find online is bad, you're going to need to start getting positive things up there. You're going to need to start writing and publishing positive, constructive pieces, if you can. You're going to want to be featured for doing good things. You're going to want to want to have good things said about you and by you up there on the internet. That is easier to do if you are a writer or have a high profile. If not, you may want to hire a firm that does reputation management. But the best way to ensure good things are out there is to do good things, make sure they're noticed, and to write and produce as much as you can that is positive, constructive, and unassociated with your mobbing.

When my mobbing commenced, I discovered that under Rate My Prof, someone had added fake reviews of classes I never taught—as if to create evidence contrary to the excellent objective reviews I had. I knew the reviews were fake because I had always checked them every semester and they hadn't been there before the mobbing, they were from classes that didn't exist and were ostensibly taught years before, and were scathing and completely contrary to all other reviews. I had no doubt that someone associated with my current employer wanted to create a new cyber-trail.

By Googling myself I've discovered comments left on blogs and forums about my case, I've discovered supporters I didn't know I had, and I've discovered crazy haters who have never met me. And by Googling my colleagues who mobbed me, I discovered one had been arrested for a serious sex crime, another had taken credit for a huge project that I had done, and a third had published something I wrote under his own name. Google. Every month. And take screenshots when you find something before it is removed (it is very difficult to get Google to remove things, but people often write things on Facebook or Twitter that they later delete, so get a screen shot).

Shred everything. If you think they won't go through your trash, think again. There's no faster way to learn about a person than to go through their trash, so shred everything. Shred every note, every scrap of paper, and every piece of junk mail—at work and at home. Especially if you find yourself embroiled in a lawsuit, you need to protect yourself. It's perfectly legal for your employer—or a private investigator they've hired—to drive up to your home in the middle of the night on the eve of your garbage collection, and empty the contents of your trashcan into their own garbage bags and drive away. As long as you've put the trash out on the curb and off your property, it's theirs (and even if it's on your property, what's going to stop them from taking it?).

Think about it. From the contents of your trash can they might find out what you've been scrawling in those notebooks. They might find out what attorneys you've contacted, what jobs you've applied for, what purchases you've made, what and how much you're drinking, and what affairs you might be having. No matter how honest and law-abiding you are, protect yourself by shredding everything at home and at work, with a cross-cut paper shredder. At the very least, it will make them wonder what you're up to.

Avoid using the word "will." Every time you use the word "will" in a communication with your employer or coworkers in regard to a conflict, unless it is an assurance you will do something work related, it's going to work against you. It signals intent, which if you do not follow through with, weakens you. It signals a threat, which provokes them into a defensive position, which for them means offense. It signals strategy, which weakens you as they conceal their strategy from you. Never tell them what you'll do until after you have done it. Don't tell them you will file anything, report anything, sue them, embarrass them, expose them, conquer them or screw them. I get emails all the time from people who feel completely powerless and do not want to give up their "will" and insist on letting their employers have it. But I'm telling you, it *will* weaken you. If you must do something, take them by surprise.

Do not make threats, even in jest. Closely associated with the use of the word "will" is the perception of a threat. Do not threaten to report your employer to anyone. Do not threaten to file a grievance if you aren't treated better. Do not threaten to sue your employer. As I said above, if you are going to do any of these things, just do it. But don't alert anyone— that is perceived as a threat, and you will be accused of "making threats."

Once you are perceived as "making threats" and mobbing commences and you become anguished and depressed and furious, it takes little effort for the "threats" to be exaggerated. Anguish and depression become portrayed as suicidal tendencies, and anger becomes portrayed as physical threats, if not homicidal tendencies. Both reinforce perceptions you are mentally unstable and a danger.

If you do become suicidal, do not, under any circumstances, express your suicidal thoughts to anyone at work, not even (especially) your closest friends. Seek help, by all means, but under no circumstances express any thoughts of suicide or self-harm to anyone associated with your workplace or profession. No one at work will help you if you are being mobbed, but they will spread gossip about it, and you will be described as "threatening" suicide. Do not even make the remark in jest, because it will be treated as a real "threat"—and the response may be so cruel that it does drive you to suicide.

Similarly, under no circumstances allow your anger to be openly expressed. Do not make jokes about wanting to kill the bastards, or hurt them in any way, no matter how much you might trust the person you're confiding in. As I write these words, there is a teenager out on bail for making a joke on an internet site about going on a shooting spree—the comment was clearly a joke in response to something someone said, and even followed by a notation he was joking. But he was jailed for several months, beaten up and kept in isolation, and is facing a lengthy prison sentence if convicted.

So do not make jokes, and under no circumstances, actually threaten to hurt anyone. You will not only lose your job, but if you have a retaliation case against an employer, they can legally fire you for such comments. Remember how gossip operates and understand that context and humor will be stripped of anything you say in its retelling. It's no joking matter.

And under no circumstances, do not hurt yourself or anyone. Your life matters, whether your coworkers and employer recognize that fact or not. There is no employer worth losing your life over. And there is certainly no justification for violence against your employer. Get out and get help if it gets that far, and by all means, get rid of any guns you might have.

Tape everything and tell no one. Just as your employer may well be secretly taping you, if you have the legal right to tape your employer, do so. But under no circumstances tell them, or tell anyone other than your attorney that you're doing so. (The exception is, if you are being questioned in a formal interview, such as in an investigation, you may want to ask permission to tape record it. At the same time, always ask them if they are tape recording you.)

Before you begin secretly taping anyone, be sure you are complying with the law. First, check the laws of your state to determine whether or not it is legal to tape record someone without their knowledge. A Google of "tape recording laws" should tell you what you need to know, but be sure to check the date of any document you find—these laws can change, so if it isn't within the last year or two, you may not want to rely on it. After typing in your search term, under "search tools" click "past year." That will get you more timely information.

If it is a two-party consent state, that means that both (or all) parties to a conversation must know they are being recorded. If that is the case, any recording you make cannot be used in court, and you might even face legal charges if you are caught.

If the law in your state indicates that it is a one-party state, that means that as long as one party to the conversation (you) knows the tape recording is being made, it is acceptable. That doesn't mean you can record someone else's conversation that you are not a party to, but it does mean that you can secretly record any conversation to which you are a party.

Be sure that if this is the case, it also applies to telephone conversations. If you can legally tape record telephone conversations without the other party's consent, then any interactions you must have with your manager and/or coworkers that you suspect will include lies, establish what you've been told, or demonstrate your or their state of mind, may well be best handled in a phone call—which you are taping.

To tape record a conversation in person, there are many small electronic recorders with excellent sound that can be slipped into a pocket or purse. Black is usually better than silver as it is less noticeable. If there is a light that is lit up when in recording mode, conceal it (you can cover it with dark nail polish, but then you won't necessarily know if you're recording or not.

If you have a smart phone, make sure that any recording you make can be downloaded onto your computer. If there is a limit to how long the recording can be, you will need to download a recording app that will enable you to record lengthy conversations. The downside to recording with a smart phone is that you have to turn it on first; what you want is a voice-activated recording that will only record when there is a conversation to record. The VR+ app has clear audio with a voice-activated feature and only costs $2.99.

To record telephone conversations, there is an app for the iPhone called Call Recorder. If you do not have an iPhone or want to record calls made from your work phone, you can find a phone recorder for about $20 that works with tape recording, or one that can be plugged into your MP3 recorder and stuck into your ear, and it will record perfectly (and should be under twenty bucks).

Now, here's the thing about surreptitious recording. First, you can't tell a sole, other than your attorney. The minute you do, you can bet that sooner or later there will be no further phone calls or conversations with your employers or coworkers. Second, even if the recording is legal and admissible in court, people don't tend to trust people who secretly record others. Employment conflicts are increasingly including recorded evidence, but there remains a stigma against those who use them. Consider surreptitious recording a tool, but only one to be used when and if it is absolutely necessary.

Keep a daily record and keep it short and simple. Once a workplace conflict begins to brew, it is essential to keep a record in which you record any adverse events, accomplishments, and emotions. At the same time, you must be very careful that you do not rant and rave in your writing or write lengthy tomes. Not only does doing so expose you to saying foolish things that will be used against you (in surprisingly ingenious ways), but it keeps your pain alive. Remember in Chapter Six where I explained how venting and discussing the abuses make you relive them? Well it can become the same with writing about them. In some cases, writing about them can be therapeutic, but it's probably best to save the therapeutic writing for when you are well past the acute pain. To safeguard any potential legal case and your sanity, keep it brief. Think of your workplace record like a Twitter account. Keep the entries factual, to the point, and concise. Something like this:

Interactions: *Met with X in his office at 10:15; he said my work was inadequate and I must improve. I asked what was inadequate about my work and he said I should know the reason and he wouldn't discuss it further. Tried to get clarification, but he refused. His secretary was present but said nothing. Returned to office, closed door and cried. I have no idea what is inadequate about my work.*
Communications: *Sent email inquiry to Affirmative Action Office re: status of investigation; received reply from Mrs. Q indicating they still have to interview witnesses.*
Events: *Group lunch at noon, X, Y and Z attended; I was not invited. Ate alone.*
Walked down hallway and all heads turned away; doors closed as my footsteps approached; said hello to W but she ignored me. At 2pm found note in my mailbox calling me crazy slut. Stored it with the others.
Achievements: *Finished Jones Report; t/c's [telephone calls] to clients; dictated first draft of memo to ABC.*
Emotions: *hurt, worried about job, very high stress, hard to concentrate*

Notice how this entry is organized to record who you spoke to at work, what happened and who witnessed it; who you wrote emails or other written communications to and who sent them to you; what nasty pranks or cruel social responses you endured; what you got done at work; and how you were feeling. By separating the entries in this way you discipline yourself to remain focused; you are better able to respond to any potential interrogatories (if it makes it as far as a lawsuit) or queries from investigators because you can provide them with clear and identifiable times and places of who you spoke with and what was said; you are able to clearly demonstrate that you are trying to get your work done despite the stress and that you are productive and valuable to the organization; and that you are suffering emotional duress.

At the same time, it prevents you from rambling about all the many small injustices, and all the emotionally crushing thoughts that are raging through your head. It makes you look less crazy, less paranoid, less focused on trivia and details, and less consumed by the politics of the workplace because you are trying to get your work done. It also limits you from saying things that might seem perfectly reasonable and accurate, but could bite you in the ass once the other side starts twisting it.

Make sure each entry is clearly dated, and that any meetings or events include the time they happened. If you mention any emails or communications, print them out and store them in a notebook, preferably labeled to correspond to the entry. If you take pictures of anything, be sure you note that you did so and that the photos are easily assessable and clearly labeled.

If the entry is a hard copy, be sure it is kept with you at all times or in a locked place where only you have access to it. Do not tell others you are keeping a record, unless an investigator or attorney asks. If you must turn over copies of your hard-copy record, be sure you retain the original (unless your attorney requests the original, in which case be sure to keep a copy).

If you are keeping the record in electronic format, be sure that it is password protected. Do not just password protect your electronic device, but password protect the diary itself.

Slowly and discretely, remove personal items from your office or work station. Whenever someone has filed a claim against an employer, whether internally or in the courts, the potential for being escorted off the premises is heightened. More and more often employers are being encouraged to publicly escort any terminated employee off premises and without notice, and when they do, the employee is publicly humiliated. You cannot ensure that this won't happen to you no matter how law abiding and loyal an employee you are. But should it happen, you can minimize the spectacle by making sure the only thing you will be seen walking out with is your purse or briefcase.

Once it becomes clear that your employer wants you gone, begin removing personal items from your workspace, little by little. Do not do it openly or drastically. Doing so would then give rise to rumors, if not accusations, that you are quitting. Just slip something (of your own) into your bag or briefcase every evening when you leave. If your workspace is very public and you don't want your depersonalization to be too obvious, you can replace a photo with an impersonal inspirational quote, something you can walk away from.

Although you cannot remove files that belong to your employer, any work product that belongs to you can be removed, and if you are unsure whose property it is, ask your lawyer or assume it belongs to your employer. You want to be sure you are never accused of taking your employer's property, but you also do not want your employer taking your property. To remove large boxes of your personal property, you can make a point of saying you are going to be doing some work over the weekend so seeing you take a box of files does not raise eyebrows, but only as long as doing so is common practice and the files belong to you and not your employer.

If you have furniture, appliances, rugs, paintings or other large items that must be removed, if you can remove them after hours or on weekends, do so. If you can't, mention you are redecorating a room at home, you need to make a repair, or someone else is in need of the item. Be casual and cheerful, and do not take everything all at once if you can avoid it. Slowly and systematically removing your personal items, while maintaining your workspace and not letting it appear abandoned, will not only help prevent the humiliation of a public escort as you carry your box of photos and awards away, but it will also give you a psychological edge by helping you to feel that you are breaking away from them, rather than they are forcing you out. You will feel sad taking these items home, but the more you do it, the more you will feel that doing so is empowering you, rather than humiliating you. And if your conflict is ultimately resolved down the road, you can always bring the items back as slowly and systematically as you removed them.

One word of caution, though: your employer may well have cameras in your office, your cubicle, the corridors, or anywhere. Assume you are on camera as you remove items. Make it clear the items are personal ones, and move naturally. You do not want a video appearing to show you stealing something, when all you were doing was stealthily slipping your own property into your briefcase. Make sure if there are cameras about, that the item you slip into that case is viewable. And always note in your journal or calendar what you took home.

Be productive. And don't beat yourself up if you're not. Finally, after all is said and done, the most important thing you can do is be productive. It is also one of the most impossible things you can do when you are being mobbed.

Some people have no problem burying themselves in their work when they are under stress, and if you are one of those people, you're blessed. Yet even the most productive workers find that the emotional and professional toll of mobbing can be more than they can withstand, and their work suffers. For many, work becomes impossible because the constancy of attack and exclusion and humiliation that one faces at work beats them down— and it is intended to beat you down.

Your employer knows that you will not be able to produce as much as your coworkers if you have to answer to one trumped up investigation after another, no longer have access to the resources necessary to do your job and have zero support from your coworkers and support staff.

They know if they keep excluding you, investigating you, scrutinizing you, insulting you, and ridiculing you, that you will not be able to produce as much as the dimwit down the hall who can't tell the difference between a job and a nap. They would rather give that dimwit a raise and an avalanche of praise than treat you with dignity and respect. That's what mobbing is all about. By beating you down, you become the unproductive, confused, emotionally damaged person that they insist you are.

To hell with them. Just remember, **as much as you fear and resent what they're thinking of you, the truth is, they're really just thinking about themselves**. And that gives you time to get busy. You need to produce right now as if your life depends upon it, in order to keep your mind off what's going on, in order to limit the ease with which they can get rid of you, and in order to make yourself employable somewhere else. So focus on the techniques in Chapter 6 for controlling your thoughts and emotions.

But avoid taking any medication designed to make you more productive such as Adderall, which is an amphetamine (speed), or Ritalin, which is a chemical clone of cocaine. Both drugs will intensify your anxiety and phobias and are probably the worse drugs you can take when you are under attack. Take anti-depressants if you need them, but learn to gain control of your thinking and your emotions and work harder than you've ever worked before.

And if you can't do that, then don't beat yourself up. There are enough people beating you up and the last thing you need is to join them in the chorus of chants that say you're no good. Do your best and work as hard as you possibly can, but above all, be tender with yourself. Be kind to yourself. And be forgiving of yourself.

But at the same time, believe in yourself. Believe in your own capacity to do your job and to do it well, whether it is with your current employer or your next one. But whatever you do, don't buy into any labels or roles that cast you as incapable of working and working hard. You may have been a target for someone else's fears and insecurities and cruelty and aggression.

But you are nobody's victim. You are nobody's road kill. You will survive. And you will thrive, if you learn to gain control of your thoughts and your emotions, and turn the nightmare of mobbing into a lesson in surviving life's unexpected cruelties and losses.

Now get to work.

Conclusion

I f there's one message I hope you have gotten from this book it is that mobbing isn't something only bad people or psychopaths or bullies do, but that it's something that everybody does. Mobbing is a human response to perceived threat. But just because it's human doesn't mean that it's humane.

If you have been bullied or mobbed at work or in any group setting where you once enjoyed being a valued member, you know firsthand how devastating and debilitating it can be. You also know how enraging it can be to be falsely accused, openly abused, and maybe even had your livelihood damaged or destroyed. You know how soul-crushing it can be to be ostracized and shunned, and for those whose shunning lasts years, or who have been blackballed as a result of the lies told about them, every new day brings the sharp pain of reminder that the life they once had is gone.

I know the feeling. When my former employers wrote to my attorneys that they would ensure I was shunned by my national colleagues, they meant it. Although I never once violated any ethical guidelines, much less any laws, and had had an excellent record and reputation beforehand, once my employers took aim and doled out raises, early tenure and grade changes to those who would assist them, none of the past two decades of my professional success amounted to anything. I was left an unemployable single mother at the age of fifty. It hurts.

But if there was anything I learned from the experience, it was that I was not and am not the person they said I was. I was not any of the cruel things they said I was, other than I allowed my emotions and anger to be expressed at a time when they were out to get me. I didn't learn to "keep my mouth shut" as so many cautioned. I didn't learn to "lay low." And I didn't learn for the longest time to "just move on," because I had no place to move to once they blackballed me.

But I did learn that had I kept my mouth shut, laid low, and moved on when I still could, that I would still have a career. I learned that had I let go of my anger at the early offenses and laughed off the minor insults, I never would have been mobbed and endured the major offenses and insults. But once mobbed, if I had kept my anguish and my fury to myself and not trusted my closest friends at work to understand the hell I was living through, I would still have a career.

Instead, I lost it all, and in the years since I settled my lawsuit against my employer, I remain shunned by my profession and former friends and colleagues. I remain unemployable and unwelcomed in my field—not for anything I ever did, but for what people *think* I did.

That's how powerful gossip is, and that's how damaging mobbing is.

Yet by applying my anthropological expertise to a study of how and why mobbing happens, and after speaking with and interviewing hundreds of mobbing targets from all over the world, I have learned that happiness may come easier with a weekly paycheck, but even if everything has been lost, we still have the capacity to feel joy each and every day. And we still have the capacity to live again and make new friends—friends who genuinely care about us.

And I have learned that mobbing completely defies nearly everything that we have been taught about "bullying."

First, as most mobbing targets come to discover, few interpersonal "bullying" encounters come close to the devastation of collective mobbing. I don't think there's a one of us who wouldn't trade the mob for a measly bully. If you are being harassed by a single individual, do your very best to handle it—and to handle yourself, including your emotions and your reactions. Do not allow that individual to influence your coworkers because once you are confronting a mob, "bullying" is not your problem. Dwelling on the psychology of "psychopaths" or "narcissists" isn't going to do you much good. You need to understand group psychology and organizational cultures if you want to diffuse the aggression. Once you do, you'll see that an entirely different dynamic takes hold once a bully turns into a mob.

Second, one of the reasons I was so unprepared for the extreme aggression that came my way was because when it first started, I relied on the bullying literature which assured me that only bad people bully and good people stand up against them. So I trusted the good people. As I now know, and as you now know, good people act badly when leadership tells them to. If you do not understand this simple fact, you are vulnerable to misjudging the people around you, and stumbling into a fire you won't be able to put out.

Third, the pain of losing everything and having been accused of horrific crimes has taught me to be introspective. It has forced me to look at some things about my own personality that turned people off, annoyed them, frightened them, or gave them the desire to hurt me and the willingness to leave me and my daughter destitute. I did not for a second deserve the hurt they inflicted, and I sure didn't deserve the shunning and destruction of my career, but that doesn't mean I cannot benefit from taking a long, hard, objective and compassionate look within.

The bullying literature that assures you that you did nothing to bring it on is no different than the saleswoman who tells you that you look great in that outfit that makes you look ridiculous. It might please you to hear it, but it isn't doing anything to help you.

Finally, as I read the bullying literature, I found time and time again it encourages people to mob others. If a person is considered a "bully" we have been advised to shun them, spread gossip about them, tell people they are bullies and elicit stories of their "bullying" behavior from others and record every single thing they do that we don't like. These things are precisely what happens in a mobbing. If the solution to bullying behaviors is to encourage hatred and mobbing, then it is no solution at all. It is a green light for aggression.

The number one thing that each and every worker can do to improve the workplace—including workers who are currently targets of mobbing and bullying—is to treat other people with kindness and compassion. Do not be mean. Do not resort to name-calling or labeling. Do not pathologize people. Do not gossip. Do not insult people you disagree with. Do not ostracize your coworkers. Do not convince yourself that just because everyone else is doing it, that it's okay if you do.

If you aren't yet being mobbed, but you certainly are being bullied, understand first and foremost that there is more to the "bully" than just their bad behavior. Show compassion, whether it comes easy or not. Focus on their good qualities, rather than their bad—but don't overlook their capacity to be hurtful. Here's an example.

I once had a job where I had to work for someone who was very petty and bitchy. I could be criticized for the most trivial things, or expected to smear others and be praised for doing so. It was a constant game of walking on eggshells—would I be read the Riot Act for an honest mistake, or would it be laughed off? Would I receive credit for what I worked so hard to accomplish, or would my boss take the credit? When she made a big mistake, would I be the one to be blamed, or would my coworker?

I desperately wanted to quit, but I couldn't. I needed the job and there were few others available at that time. So I made up my mind that I would focus on my boss's good qualities, and ignore the bad ones.

My boss, petty and bitchy perhaps, was also extremely generous. She was bright. She had a good sense of humor. She helped a lot of people with their careers and with their personal lives. She had survived a lot of discriminatory treatment in the past and built a solid career late in life. She had a difficult spouse, but managed to make a strong marriage. She had principles, which perhaps got buried by the petty and bitchy behaviors.

In short, there was a lot about my boss—who some would have easily classified as "a bully"—that made me know that we could work together.

So I focused only on those good qualities, and every time the pettiness and bitchiness reared its ugly head, I learned to laugh it off or ignore it, and focus on the good stuff.

And what do you know, the good stuff just got better. And the job just got better. And to this day, she was one of the best bosses I ever had— despite the negatives.

Flash forward a whole lot of years and I was working once again for someone I'd easily classify as "a bully." I did what I had done for years since learning my lesson to look at their good side. And this new boss did have many good qualities. He, too, was intelligent. And he worked hard, and he could be very supportive. So when he behaved badly, I reminded myself that he had good qualities, and that these good qualities would prevail.

But they didn't. I made the mistake of inflating his good qualities, and overly ignoring his capacity to hurt people—and the visible delight that showed on his face when he did so. I watched as he smiled when he did something to hurt people, but I didn't register it. I knew he was a prick, but I figured if I treated him with respect and focused on his good qualities, everything would be fine just as it was with my former boss.

The critical difference, however, was that while my other boss had some negative qualities, as we all do, they didn't bring her pleasure. Sure, the snide gossip always did, but she didn't have a vengeful streak, and she didn't delight in punishing people. She could be unpredictable, temperamental and petty, but she wasn't mean-spirited and didn't take joy in her bad behaviors.

This other boss did, however; the red flags were there, but I ignored them.

Had I focused on his good qualities, over his bad, which I did do, but at the same time taken his capacity and desire to cause pain seriously, I would have been better served. It would have been disastrous to have called him a bully to anyone, to have confronted him, to have reported him, or to have done anything to challenge him.

But had I heeded the red flags, such as the small delights he took in doling out punishments, I also would have realized that when there was a conflict at work, going to him for help was a suicidal maneuver. He was a Worried Killer. He was a man who had been beaten down and controlled by more powerful men, then put in charge of others. He was a man who had been given the capacity to hurt others, and come to enjoy it. And he was a man who would never let anyone bring conflict to his world that he didn't define and control himself.

So what does all this mean for you?

It means that if someone is bullying you, do what you can to diffuse the conflict, but focus on their good qualities. Understand that when it comes to the people we call "bullies" that one size does not fit all. There are all sorts of people in this world, and all sorts of aggressive people. Focus on their good qualities, learn to laugh off as much as you can, and be as productive and agreeable as you can. *But do not ignore the red flags and do not become a victim.*

Do not cower, do not walk with your shoulders hung down, do not wince and weep. Keep your pride, and keep your emotional cool. Understand that sometimes you're a drag to be around as well.

Is the person you think is "a bully" someone who is just abrasive and may not even know it? Or do they genuinely enjoy their power and their ability to wound others? If you are dealing with someone who enjoys hurting other people, or someone who sweeps their ethics under the rug the moment that it suits them, be cautious with what information you share, be cautious about bringing any concerns, conflicts or workplace issues to them, and keep your distance while remaining cordial. Do not gossip about them, do not demonize them, and do not join in a mob against them. Just be friendly, and beware.

At the same time, recognize that no one "bully" is really your biggest problem. Your biggest problem is your inability to control your emotions, adjust your expectations and perceptions, and successfully negotiate the social landmines—but the good news is, that's something you can learn. Your biggest problem is that until and unless you learn how to do these things, there remains the possibility that one bully could turn into a mob. Your coworkers have the capacity to hurt you, and some will be more likely to do so than others.

The people closest to you have the capacity to do you the most harm. In the event someone in a position of leadership wants you out, be especially careful around them—but also, don't push them into a corner by expecting too much from them. They'll let you down if you do so, turn on you if you press it, but possibly help you if you step away until and unless they're ready.

Be especially wary of the ambitious colleague; we are all ambitious, but some are more so than others. Do not be blinded by their stated principles, their religious devotion, or their political allegiance. None of those things will matter if they decide that for any reason you are in the way of their advancement and/or that your elimination would provide them opportunities.

Be wary of junior colleagues—those who have less status and/or are newcomers to the workplace. They will be expected to prove themselves, are easiest to fire, and this is an opportunity for them to not only prove themselves, but to leapfrog over you.

Be especially wary of those closest to any source of institutional power, by way of their position or their personal relationships with those in power. In a mobbing context, they are far more likely to do you harm than good, so keep your distance.

Be especially wary of the gossips, the chronic complainers, and the "concerned" acquaintances who pump you for information.

But most of all, be especially wary of yourself, because if you are being mobbed, you are constantly doubting yourself. You are frightened and furious and not at your best and not making good decisions. Be gentle and tender with yourself, and do everything you can to survive. Don't wage war, don't raise hell and don't demand justice—no matter how strongly you believe in fighting for those principles. In the workplace, those are losing battles, but if you survive or avoid a mobbing, you will find yourself in the position to promote justice and a healthier work environment from a stronger and safer vantage point. You cannot attain justice when you're standing in the center of a bulls-eye.

Be strong. Be calm. And above all, be kind.

And seek laughter, wherever and whenever you can find it. Life is far too short to be spent in a battle with bullies, with mobs or with ourselves.

And if you do lose the battle, you'll still recover, even if it leaves you blinded and maimed and scrambling around on the floor for the head they knocked off your neck.

You can recover.

But only if you take the lead in your own healing process. So start right now on controlling your obsessive thinking. Learn to gain control of your thoughts, and you will gain control of your emotions.

And once you have gained control of your emotions, you'll have greater control over the mob and over your future.

It doesn't start with any bully.

It starts with you.

References

Allport, Gordon W. and Leo Postman (1947) *The Psychology of Rumor* Oxford, England: Henry Holt.

Bing, Stanley (2000) *What Would Machiavelli Do? The Ends Justify the Meanness* New York: HarperBusiness.

Crombag, H. F. M., Wagenaar, W. A., and van Koppen, P. J. (1996) Crashing Memories and the Problem of 'Source Monitoring. *Applied Cognitive Psychology, 10*, 95-104.

Frontline (1985) *A Class Divided*, available online at: http://www.pbs.org/wgbh/pages/ frontline/shows/divided/etc/view.html

Garner, Helen (1995/1997) *The First Stone: Some Questions About Sex and Power.* New York: The Free Press.

Gawande, Atul (2009) "Hellhole: The United States Holds Tens of Thousands of Inmates in Long Term Solitary Confinement. Is This Torture?" March 30, 2009, *The New Yorker,* available online at: http://www.newyorker.com/reporting/2009/03/30/090330fa_fact_gawande

Goodall, Jane (1977) Infant Killing and Cannibalism in Free-Living Chimpanzees, *Folia Primatologica*, 28:259-282.

Harlow, Harry F., R. O. Dodsworth and M. K. Harlow, (1965) "Total Social Isolation in Monkeys," *Proceedings of the National Academy of Science, U.S.A.*, available online at: http://www.ncbi.nlm.nih.gov/pmc/articles/PMC285801/pdf/pnas00159-0105.pdf

Hillard, James Randolph (2009) "Workplace Mobbing: Are They Really Out to Get Your Patient?" *Current Psychiatry* 8:4:45-51, available online at: http://www.currentpsychiatry.com/ fileadmin/cp_archive/pdf/0804/0804CP_Article4.pdf

Hölzel BK, Carmody J, Vangel M, et al. (2011) Mindfulness practice leads to increases in regional brain gray matter density. *Psychiatry Research: Neuroimaging.* 191(1):36–43. Available through the National Institute of Health (NIH) at: http://nccam.nih.gov/research/results/spotlight/012311.htm

Lawrence, R. D. (1986) *In Praise of Wolves*, New York: Henry Holt and Company.

Leymann, Heinz (1990) *Psychological Reactions to Violence in Working Life*, Umeå, 1990 (Umeå University medical dissertations, 0346-6612; N.S., 289).

Loftus, E. F., & Palmer, J. C. (1974) Reconstruction of Auto-Mobile Destruction: An Example of the Interaction Between Language and Memory. *Journal of Verbal Learning and Verbal Behaviour*, 13:585-589.

Loftus, Elizabeth, and J. E. Pickrell (1995) "The Formation of False Memories, *Psychiatric Annals* 25:720–725, available online at: http://users.ecs.soton.ac.uk/harnad/Papers/Py104/loftusmem1.pdf

Lorenz, Konrad (1963) *On Aggression*, New York: Routledge.

Maestripieri, Dario (2007) *Macachiavellian Intelligence: How Rhesus Macaques and Humans Have Conquered the World*. Chicago and London: University of Chicago Press.

Milgram, Stanley (1963) "Behavioral Study of Obedience," *Journal of Abnormal and Social Psychology* 67(4):371–8.

Niehoff, Debra (1998) *The Biology of Violence: How Understanding the Brain, Behavior, and Environment Can Break the Vicious Circle of Aggression*, New York: The Free Press.

Olsen, Gary (2008) "Avoiding Academe's Ax Murderers," *Chronicle of Higher Education*, October 15, 2008, available online at: http://chronicle.com/article/Avoiding-Academe-s-Ax/45794

Porter, Phil (2000) *Eat or Be Eaten: Jungle Warfare for the Master Corporate Politicia*, Paramus, NJ: Prentice Hall.

Randles, Daniel, S. J. Heine, and N. Santos (2013) "The Common Pain of Surrealism and Death: Acetaminophen Reduces Compensatory Affirmation Following Meaning Threats," *Psychological Science* 24(6):966-973.

Roth, Philip (2000) *The Human Stain*, New York: Vintage Books.

Schrijvers, Joep P. M. (2004) *The Way of the Rat: A Survival Guide to Office Politics*, London: Cyan Books (Translated by Jonathan Ellis).

Williams, Kipling (2001) *Ostracism: The Power of Silence*, New York and London: The Guilford Press.

Zimbardo, Philip (2007) *The Lucifer Effect: Understanding How Good People Turn Evil*, New York: Random House.

Resources

The resources available to targets of bullying are vast and can easily be found with a bit of Googling. The resources for targets of mobbing, however, are much more limited. But here are some websites and books that should be helpful to you.

Websites
The Mobbing Portal http://www.mobbingportal.com/
The Mobbing Portal is a website under the direction of sociologist Kenneth Westhues. Professor Westhues is the leading authority on academic mobbing, and although the Portal is not updated regularly (it appears the latest news is from 2009), it provides many cases of mobbing, and offers a list of resource articles, resources for teachers, police officers, nurses and academics, as well as a blog (which also hasn't been updated since 2009). It is well worth checking out, particularly if you are an academic.

Workplace Mobbing in Academe
http://www.arts.uwaterloo.ca/~kwesthue/mobbing.htm
This is Kenneth Westhues's site exclusively devoted to academic mobbing. He provides case stories and resources which, though focused on academic mobbing, are relevant to all mobbing targets in many respects.

Mobbing USA: Emotional Abuse in the American Workplace
http://www.mobbing-usa.com/
A Canadian site with many articles, case studies and resources for mobbing targets.

Mobbing-CA http://members.shaw.ca/mobbing/mobbingCA/index.htm
Overcome Bullying http://www.overcomebullying.org/workplace-bullying-book.html
Mobbing-CA and Overcome Bullying are both run by Anton Hout, a Canadian journalist who has been writing about workplace bullying and mobbing for several years. His sites provide a wealth of information on mobbing and bullying, and his own edited volume, *What Every Target of Workplace Bullying Needs to Know*, on how to overcome mobbing and bullying are available on either site.

Our Bully Pulpit www.ourbullypulpit.com
A site run by filmmaker Beverly Peterson, Our Bully Pulpit is updated regularly and provides resources, articles, blog posts and videos on the topic of bullying and mobbing.

Workplace Violence News
http://workplaceviolencenews.com/2011/10/05/what-every-target-of-workplace-bullying-needs-to-know/
Another Canadian site with a great deal of information, Workplace Violence News is run by three former corporate security professionals, Ross Arrowsmith, Dick Bevan and Helen Jensen. Although focused on bullying rather than mobbing, and primarily aimed at organizations rather than targets, it is still a useful resource for anyone concerned about workplace aggression.

Heinz Leymann http://www.leymann.se/English/frame.html
A site established by the late Professor Heinz Leymann, who introduced the concept of workplace mobbing. It is a bit overwhelming initially, and more

of a book in itself rather than a website, but to anyone interested in the topic of mobbing, it is well worth reading.

Bully Blocking http://www.bullying.com.au
A website by psychologist and public speaker Evelyn M. Field who presents a more reasoned approach to dealing with the problem of workplace bullying. Although not specific to mobbing targets, Dr. Field's approach to the problem is helpful to anyone enduring workplace, school or community aggression. She distinguishes between intentional, serial, bullying and ordinary people who become caught up in it, acknowledging that a great deal of bullying is perpetrated by ordinary people who are responding in a specific context in which leadership encourages shunning and bullying. She also offers a number of books on bullying, which I have not yet read, but do look promising.

For Whistleblowers

For anyone who works for the U.S. or Canadian governments and has blown a whistle (or is thinking of doing so), the following two sites are invaluable. Fair Whistle Blower is a Canadian site and Peer is a U.S.-based site, but both are excellent resources for whistleblowers.

> http://fairwhistleblower.ca/wbers/wb_bullying.html
> http://www.peer.org/campaigns/whistleblowers/scientfiic-integrity/

Books

Despite the plethora of books on bullying, there are few books out on mobbing that are accessible to the general public. But do check them out.

Mobbing: Emotional Abuse in the American Workplace (1995 and revised in 2002 and 2005), by Noa Davenport, Ruth Distler Schwartz and Gail Pursell Elliott, Ames, Iowa: Civil Society Press.

This is a concise but helpful book that defines mobbing, provides case studies and offers suggestions on how to cope. Unfortunately, it is no longer available as of this writing, but used copies may be available.

Mobbing: Causes, Consequences, and Solutions (2012) by Maureen Duffy and Len Sperry, Oxford: Oxford University Press.

An academic book written by a psychologist (Sperry) and family therapist (Duffy), it is an excellent overview of the psychology of mobbing, focusing on the impact on targets and the organizational context in which mobbing operates. It also offers some suggestions on how targets can cope. The downside is the steep price ($55.00 on Amazon), and the academic focus, which may not appeal to many mobbing targets. If you have an interest in understanding mobbing in-depth, however, it is well researched and informative.

Overcoming Mobbing: A Recovery Guide for Workplace Aggression and Bullying, (2013), by Maureen Duffy and Len Sperry, Oxford: Oxford University Press.

Duffy and Sperry, authors of *Mobbing*, are a promising duo whose work will hopefully go far in waking the field of clinical psychology to the phenomenon of mobbing. More importantly for readers, they provide many useful suggestions for how to cope and recover from mobbing. And as someone who has long advocated a focus on workplace aggression, as opposed to just bullying, I find the title a promising start to what should become a popular book for anyone suffering from workplace aggression.

Emotional Recovery from Workplace Mobbing: A Guide for Targets and Their Supports, (2013) by Richard Schwindt, Richard Schwindt Publications.

Richard Schwindt is a Canadian social worker who works with mobbing targets and their families. He has written this popular handbook, and a companion workbook, to help people cope with and heal from the emotional traumas of mobbing. In addition to providing an overview of mobbing, he presents a number of different therapeutic techniques, and discusses at length the recovery process. Schwindt has been a tireless advocate for mobbing targets and provides creative and effective tools for healing from the trauma of mobbing, shunning and career damage.

Eliminating Professors: A Guide to the Dismissal Process (1999), by Kenneth Westhues, Edwin Mellon Press. Kenneth Westhues can be credited for bringing the concept of mobbing to North America through a series of books he has written on academic mobbing. Most are priced beyond the ordinary consumer's budget, with prices from $100 to nearly $1,000, but this title is now available in paperback for under $30.00. Written in a tongue-in-cheek style and in need of some editing (though I've only read the hardbound, not the paperback edition), it pretty much hits the nail on the head in terms of how mobbing goes down, despite veering into a rather flippant tone at times. It is written about academic mobbing, but I think many mobbing targets would find it descriptive of how mobbing unfolds in many organizations.

The Anxiety and Phobia Workbook (2011) by Edmund Bourne, New Harbinger Publications.

I first came across this book when I asked a friend in the mental health profession to recommend a book for someone who had a non-mobbing related problem with generalized anxiety. After looking it over, I felt it would be an excellent resource for anyone suffering from the anxiety and fears related to mobbing and bullying.

Another useful and free ebook is, *Managing your Anxiety & Panic Workbook*, available at:

http://www.gobookee.net/managing-your-anxiety-and-panic-workbook/

There are also other free anxiety workbooks at this link, though I haven't yet reviewed any.

Taming the Abrasive Manager (2007) by Laura Crawshaw, San Francisco: Jossey-Bass.

This book is written primarily for HR personnel, managers and others in organizations who are coping with challenging, or what the author terms "abrasive" personalities. Although not specific to mobbing and not written for targets, I find the book a breath of fresh air in the manner in which the author approaches workplace conflicts. Dispelling the notion that people are one-size-fits-all "bullies," Crawshaw tackles the problems with the bully label head on and offers a far more effective and compassionate approach to working with people whose personalities and managerial styles are causing problems at work. Rather than demonizing people labeled "bullies," she shows why abrasive managers act as they do, why they may be oblivious to the impact of their actions, and how they can change their interactions with others so that organizations can peaceably resolve conflicts and retain employees. Highly recommended to both managers and mobbing or bullying targets.

Videos

There are few documentaries on mobbing, but I highly recommend *Murder by Proxy*, a documentary about how organized bullying and shunning have led otherwise peaceful and sane workers to snap and kill people in the workplace. It is currently available on Netflix.

Another excellent documentary is Beverly Peterson's *What Killed Kevin?* Peterson set out to investigate a story about a man who committed suicide, allegedly due to a "bully boss." But once she got there, she discovered that there was little or no evidence that the victim's tragic suicide was due to "bullying," and that while there were clearly problems in the workplace, outside forces in the anti-bullying movement had intervened to shape the story as one of a "bully boss" and helpless victim. Her award-winning film is also available as an interactive feature, enabling the viewer to come to their own conclusions about what led a talented man to take his own life. It is available at http://whatkilledkevin.com/.

Acknowledgements

would like to thank the countless readers who have contacted me over the years, sharing their painful stories of workplace abuse. I would also like to thank the many colleagues who have shared not only their publications, but their own insights, experiences, expertise, and views of workplace and human aggression. We collectively represent a diversity of approaches and perceptions to a problem that concerns us all. Among those who have been especially helpful and supportive, I thank Kenneth Westhues, Beverly Peterson, and Richard Schwindt. (None are to be blamed for anything I may have written in this book; I take sole responsibility for any errors, omission or outlandish conclusions.)

There are a multitude of others whose work has influenced me, and as with any social problem or academic concern, the knowledge of a single author is the outcome of the knowledge of all those who came before, and my own work is no exception.

I would like to acknowledge my abusers and ostracizers for the lessons their own aggressive behaviors taught me. They were undeserving, cruel and mean-spirited lessons, but I am all the wiser for what I have learned, all the more clear-thinking for what I endured, and all the more at peace for what I have discovered in the solitude of safety and silence.

I am eternally grateful to K.C. Bacon, who showed me that it doesn't always take a village. Sometimes it just takes one person to turn your life around.

Finally, I thank my daughter, Mira, for her unending patience, compassion and joy. If it weren't for her, I never would have made it through the gauntlet.

About the Author

J anice Harper is a cultural anthropologist with a Ph.D. from Michigan State University. She is the author of a critically-acclaimed ethnography, *Endangered Species: Health, Illness and Death Among Madagascar's People of the Forest* (Carolina Academic Press), and has been the recipient of a number of awards and fellowships, including Fulbright, Ford Foundation and the National Science Foundation. She was a well-respected scholar of health and environment while teaching at the University of Tennessee, where she established a graduate program in Human Rights, prior to being mobbed by university administrators and junior faculty after reporting concerns about an employee's conduct toward her and other women. The mobbing that she was subjected to resulted in the university paying her a substantial settlement, and she now writes on the topic of workplace aggression for *Psychology Today* and *The Huffington Post*. More about Dr. Harper can be found at her website, www.janice-harper.com.

Made in the USA
Las Vegas, NV
15 March 2022

45651059R00134